Golf Psyche
Second Edition

William A. Howatt

Howatt HR Consulting Inc.

ISBN 978-1-894338-80-6

Published 2007

Editing, typesetting, and layout design by
        Al Kingsbury, A Way With Words Editorial Services

Cover design by Joan Sinclair

Graphics by Don Crowell

HOWATT HR CONSULTING INC.
6585 Hwy. 221
Kentville NS B4N 3V7

Dedicated to my wife Sherrie,

for all her patience, support and love,

and to my children, Emily, Thomas, and Patrick.

GOLF
Psyche ™

The Golf Psyche Logo

The two silhouettes of heads dominating the Golf Psyche logo represent the conscious and unconscious minds, which are the central focus of the program. Between the two silhouettes is a golf ball sitting on a tee and bracketed by two stylized swooshes, which represent the travel patterns of a well-executed golf swing and the trajectory of a ball in flight.

Foreword

HOW'S your golf game? Is your game at the level you want? If not, do you have a plan for getting there? For the last 25 years, I have struggled with this question, both as a professional golfer and as a professional golf instructor. Over the 15 years, I competed at the PGA Tour level, played in five U.S. Opens, and played six years with the PGA Tour, I adapted the Ben Hogan work ethic for improving the game. It goes like this: go out and hit a lot of balls. Then when you think you're done, hit a bunch more.

I lived and breathed golf, but my entire focus as a golfing professional was on the physical aspect of the game. It took me my entire professional career to figure out that mastering the physical part of the game, using mechanics and effort alone, was not enough to reach the very top. I saw people who had less athletic ability and spent fewer hours playing the game, win major championships repeatedly. This both frustrated and further motivated me to work even harder on my mechanics, but that only led to mental and physical fatigue. After years of competition, I finally realized the missing element of my game — the mental aspect.

To explain how I got to the point where I am today, let me share with you a brief history. I first fell in love with the game of golf back at University of North Carolina, in 1973. I was young, full of energy, motivated to play, and obsessed with the game. I took that energy and won collegiate and amateur events. Through my athleticism, I was able to achieve a high competency level, so it was a natural progression for me to turn professional in 1980, when I played my first U.S. Open event. Jack Nicklaus opened up with a 63, while I struggled to an 81.

I realized that I had to work harder to compete at that level, which furthered my Ben Hogan practice mentality, and I took this pattern into four more U.S. Opens. Working with David Leadbetter, I was able to refine my mechanics and improve my game. I continued to compete, refine my skills, and work harder, until 1991, when I was totally exhausted from travel, competing, and working so hard. I could no longer try to be Ben! I could drive, putt, and chip like a true pro; however, I was frustrated, because I didn't have a mental focus, and worse, I didn't know I needed one.

I took six months off and worked with a sports psychologist as a last-ditch effort to rescue my game. Only through patient commitment did I start to enjoy the benefits of the mental game. I was amazed at how quickly the development occurred. I could mentally put myself in "the zone." My energy was rekindled to compete with these new skills, making my game complete; however, at this point and time in my life, due to my family commitment, I could no longer afford being away so often, competing professionally. That led me to becoming a professional golf instructor.

Now I realize how important it is to integrate the mind and body to fully develop your potential, and I took this new-found knowledge into my coaching and golfing. I read and researched all that I could about the mental part of the game, because I knew that training the mind was integral to helping the body perform to a new standard of excellence.

In my quest, I came across an innovative process called Golf Psyche. I am excited about Golf Psyche's path to the Golf Zone and its value as a new tool that helps coach and student define all aspects of the game.

Golf Psyche is a program that focuses on teaching the golfer how to get the conscious mind out of the way, so the unconscious mind, which executes the golf swing, can perform to the body's full potential. The process provides a vehicle for the golfer to set up the conscious mind to train the unconscious mind. From looking at a lot of mental programs, I have come to the decision that Golf Psyche is the new sensation for mental preparation. This book comes with a tremendous number of mental tools, combined into one easy-to-follow program. It provides a way for the golfer to find balance between the mental and physical parts of the game. I believe the difference between the champions of golf and good golfers is the grasp of the mental game. I know champions have a great deal of physical ability or they would never have reached the top. However, the key to their success, in my opinion, is how they are able to balance both the mental and physical parts of the game.

Many golfers can perform when the game is just for fun, but the difference between good golfers and champions is the ability to play well regardless of the stakes. In other words, they are able to keep their minds focused and balanced under pressure. I am truly excited about adding the element of Golf Psyche to my students' golf game. This program will teach you how to get the most of your mind when you are dedicated and committed to developing your golf game. As with all mental game training, there is a learning curve of about 50 days. You will learn to enjoy the benefits that come from focusing on the mental exercises as much as you would physically gripping and ripping a driver.

As with anything in life, those who are focused and disciplined will achieve greater results. Congratulations on taking a step to becoming the best golfer that you can be and taking your golf game to the next level. I wish you good luck on your mental journey with Golf Psyche.

— *William Buttner, PGA Professional*

Course layout

Warmup

EVERY golfer who has played more than a few rounds knows there is more to this game than the physical act of hitting a ball and sending it soaring towards a green, or tapping a putt and confidently watching it roll slowly to the cup. Like all athletes, golfers know that their emotional state and mental attitude probably have as much or more to do with their score as the hours spent on the practice tee. If I can hit the ball successfully one time, and seemingly do no wrong throughout a round today, why can't I do the same tomorrow, is a question they continually ask.

As one who has loved and played the game since I was eleven years old, I have been there, and admit to being one of those who have put a few clubs in trees when shots didn't go quite right. But instead of just accepting the phenomenon of inconsistent play, I've used my years of research, study, and professional practice to bring together the power of modern-day psychological theories and deliver them to my favourite sport.

Golf Psyche is an accumulation of the most powerful mental programming techniques available. I have taken a number of theories and combined them to offer what I see as the major benefits to golfers, so they can improve their game and enjoy success on the course. Although a golfer may be totally unaware of these theories, any one of them on its own could help improve their game. Each technique has helped thousands, if not millions, of people, and now I have taken all these teachings and combined them in a unique program that is understandable, simple, and enjoyable.

The name Golf Psyche was chosen because when players win or lose at golf, it is usually due to their current state of mind. If they feel confident and determined, golf is an easy game for them, but if they are irritated and distracted, their game suffers. The purpose of Golf Psyche is to help you learn how to make the game of golf easier, so that you can believe that you are able to play at your full potential much more consistently.

For many golfers, this program will be their first experience at unleashing the power of the mind, so enjoy it; you'll not regret what you can do.

One of the major underpinnings of Golf Psyche is the importance of pure, positive thought at a conscious level. If, on a daily basis, through learning Golf Psyche, you can carry yourself with grace, sensitivity, and inner calm, you will have the greatest chance to be able to succeed and to share your success. I have seen many golfers reach short-term success and lose it, all because their conscious thought was based on self-pride, greed, and having a big ego with low moral principles.

I have concluded that being successful at golf depends on more than the obvious factors, such as practice and instruction. It hinges, to a large extent, on the power of conscious thought. My research shows that any athlete who plays golf for the primary purpose of the pride of winning, or for money will have a frustrating and short career. But the golfer who can focus on playing, not only for the thrill of winning, but also for the joy of the game, and who enjoys a sense of sharing success with others, will be the one who is consistently successful.

A golfer who develops this goodwill of sharing will be the one everyone loves to see succeed, and those who watch that golfer play will experience a sense of pure conscious energy.

This point could not be better demonstrated than it was at the 1998 Masters Tournament. Those who watched that match saw Fred Couples and Mark O'Meara cheer each other on, and late in the final round, when Couples came back to tie his lead with an impressive eagle, O'Meara was the first to greet him. One could see that O'Meara was being extremely competitive and wanting to win, but never at the expense of having a negative thought for his competitor. To witness O'Meara win the tournament with a difficult birdie putt on No. 18, and then to see Couples smile and offer congratulations, was truly a joyful experience. Either man could have won, and conscious positive thought and goodwill were in my mind as the obvious reason why one of this pair wore the coveted green jacket home.

Another example is Harvey Penick who, as he grew older, was no longer just a coach and teacher. Because he saw his students as gifts, he coached not for the pride of winning, but out of a sense of joy and love. He was grateful for his students and what they brought him, not for what he gave to them.

The power and benefits of pure conscious thought are outside our level of awareness and human understanding;however, science has shown that this power is present. The key to success in golf and in life is to comply with the forces of what we can control, and to develop a level of awareness of how truly powerful the mind can be in creating positive pure thought.

To succeed at golf, we need to stop relying just on activities that lead to an internal focus on success. When we start to focus on expecting success for total individual benefit, we are on the road to less productivity. The key to success is working hard, then being willing to share our good fortune with others.

Golf Psyche will teach you how to use your conscious mind to more effectively allow your unconscious mind to perform to its full potential. Although this program will help improve your game through focus, there is a power of consciousness that is outside our understanding and awareness that can be used to develop golf into a game of joy and peace.

Motivation for success must be based on high principles and an understanding that your gift is to be shared. We all love to see a player like Fred Couples make a hole-in-one on the most difficult 17th hole and share in the excitement and the feeling of joy that his success brings.

Golf Psyche provides the knowledge that enables you to develop a healthy conscious mind to help you become more skilled and able to maintain an internal state of sharing and kindness. It also will help you train your unconscious mind to achieve excellence in golf.

I will introduce you to three new clubs for your mental golf bag. The *Planning Club* will ensure you have a well-thought-out plan with attainable goals; the *Foundation Club* will help you put in place physical and mental pillars on which to build your game; and the *Success Club* will focus on the importance of training your conscious mind to be calm and relaxed, and for your unconscious mind to play to its potential. The benefit for you will be a better mental state for positive, pure thought.

People ask me what Golf Psyche really is. I explain it as a full mind and body integration program to excel at golf. It takes into account the following parts:

- Conscious preparation for golf success.

- Unconscious preparation for golf success.

- Understanding how to balance frustrations.

- Clearing any blocks that affect the mental part of performance.

- Stabilizing the body so it is totally balanced.

We all have individual preferences of how we like to learn. The left brainers have a need for details and structure. Right brain golfers like Fred Couples also will benefit greatly from this program, because they will develop new ways to create their magic on the course.

As with any mental program, find out what is going to push and challenge you into creating a new personal mindset for golf success, just as baseball great Mark McGwire shattered the 62 home run season record and raised the bar to a phenomenal 70. Golf Psyche can create the opportunity for you to explode through new personal barriers to golf success.

Golf is a mental game, and this program, with focus and commitment, will greatly improve your mind and body connection with the outcome of new golf success.

To be at a peak level of performance and stay there involves reasons, above and beyond your hard work, that we cannot yet comprehend. True champions are for the people, and not for themselves. If you follow Golf Psyche with a vision to share, to smile, to bring joy, and to accept that all you can do is play to your best ability, you will play like a champion and with a level of consciousness that is pure.

I believe that through work and effort golf will be more than just recording a low score. It will become a game that provides you with a true sense of joy and relaxation. At this level of consciousness and with Golf Psyche you will be enjoying golf as never before and sharing your success with others.

Best wishes, good thoughts, and improved golf!

— Bill Howatt

Tee off

D O you hit a golf ball consciously or unconsciously? To test this question, pick up a club and consciously take a practice swing.

Did you do it?

Well, you may have thought you did, but how many muscles were you aware of moving and asking to move?

Did you ask your lower back muscles to tighten and relax? Did you ask the other hundreds of muscles that you used to move? Did you consciously co-ordinate the motion?

Of course not! Once you started to swing, your conscious mind simply turned over control to your unconscious mind, which followed a set of programmed instructions for your body to make the swinging motion with the club.

The same goes for when you actually hit the ball. For example, if you need to hit a shot 98 yards to the pin, do you consciously hit the ball 98 yards, or do you take a practice swing, consciously get the feel of what 98 yards feels like, and then swing the club unconsciously? The actual 98-yard shot and its success depend on how well programmed your unconscious mind is and how your conscious mind is able to stay out of the way. So, to make the shot, you set it up and plan it.

The objective of Golf Psyche, an innovative program designed for golfers at all skill levels, is to dramatically improve your golf game by using a model that combines physical training with strong mental preparation. The practice of mental preparation can provide benefits equal to or greater than physical preparation for the game. Golf Psyche, through conscious mental and physical activity, trains the unconscious mind to play to the golfer's full potential in all kinds of conditions.

Golf Psyche has been designed using the most powerful combination of human change tools presently available. If you work at the program, your results will greatly improve your golf game, and the proof will be your lower scores.

Many golfers have the potential to greatly improve their game, but will never achieve their physical potential because they neglect to improve their mental habits. No matter how skilled you are, you cannot hit a golf shot unless you think about it and learn to be prepared. Golf Psyche is a process of learning how to condition your mind so you can move to the next level of your physical potential. It assists you to utilize the Golf Zone, to better join mind and body harmoniously with the goal of becoming the best golfer you can be, and deserve to be. Golf Psyche coaches you in removing mental obstacles of the game and conditioning your mind and body to succeed positively.

Golf Psyche believes that if you can stand up and drive a golf ball 245 yards 3 times out of 10, you should be able to do it consistently. If you can shoot even par when playing for fun, but shoot 15 over in a tournament, Golf Psyche asks, why does this happen? How can it be corrected? How can playing golf be easier?

Golf Psyche is based on the power of the unconscious mind, whose only purpose is to serve the powerful conscious mind. Through mental concentration and practice, what we think of consciously will set up our unconscious mind to deliver. When an unconscious mind is trained and conditioned, it will develop and use an ingrained blueprint to comply with what the conscious mind requests. In golf, the blueprint is the needed swing for each shot you have trained for. You will find that once you learn to trust the process, you will have confidence that your unconscious mind will be able to create the swing you need. The unconscious mind sort of builds up through conscious practice a catalogue of shots that it can draw upon when needed.

For the purpose of Golf Psyche, we are interested in developing the blueprint golf swing for a driver through to putter. The unconscious mind will develop and store the needed swing. All you need to do is learn how to condition your unconscious mind through conscious preparation to follow the blueprint. You can get your conscious mind to prepare you physically and mentally, but it is your unconscious mind that will organize the smooth integration of mind and body for golf excellence. Once you learn to trust the process, you will only need to use your conscious mind to point, decide what to do, and trust that your unconscious mind will deliver.

There are many good golfers, in the area of a 10 handicap or lower, who could greatly reduce their scores with Golf Psyche, because the biggest difference between a 10 handicapper and a scratch golfer is the self-belief in one's potential, along with the mental preparation and mental competence and belief that one can play golf to one's full potential.

Lack of mental development, rather than physical ability, is usually the factor that restricts players from improving their game, but in Golf Psyche, both aspects will be interwoven, as the importance of knowledge of the game, practice, and coaching all are stressed.

To be a 10 handicapper, a golfer must be able to strike the ball well, hitting it squarely on a drive, and have the skills to play the long iron and short iron game, as well as make the occasional difficult putt. Too many golfers focus only on the part of the game they are already good at, or want to be good at. Too often they concentrate on the long shot (the big drive), and rarely practice any mental conditioning. Golf Psyche looks at golf as a game we play both on the course and in our heads.

The lower your handicap, the more you can benefit from mental game preparation. For example, someone who has a difficult time breaking 100 needs to learn the skills of the game and get a solid and consistent swing. Golf Psyche can help speed this process, as well as improve your overall game. Those golfers who are low handicappers will greatly benefit from the mental development that Golf Psyche will provide. For golfers with good swings, the difference between winners and losers usually comes down to those who can maintain their mental discipline, focus, and concentration, and not consciously think themselves out of victory.

To be a great golfer is the same as doing anything well. It starts with the belief in yourself, and the action taken to make the belief a part of your life. For you to improve the mental part of your game, you need to want to believe in yourself, and judge yourself based on who you are as a person, not by your score. If you believe in yourself, and follow the teachings of Golf Psyche, you will experience the following golf success formula:

Physical and mental efficiency
(knowledge and skills to play golf both mentally and physically)

+   Physical and mental competency
(the necessary mental and physical skills to be able to perform at the desired level

=   Success and self-acceptance
(the belief that no matter what happens, you were prepared and played to your potential for that day)

A belief is like a golf ball. For a ball to be well driven, you need a tee for the ball to sit on and the right club to hit the ball the desired direction and distance. For our beliefs to be put in motion, our tee needs to be a desire to take action daily to become the best we can be. The club to drive our beliefs to reach our goal is confidence in our training and preparation. As you focus on being good at golf, and believe daily in what you want through healthy living, you will be in a position to control your destiny and reach your goals.

I always loved sports as a university student, and as a varsity athlete playing football, the major emphasis was on physical play, so I worked at lifting weights and gaining weight. I never looked at the mental aspect of the sport, though I always wondered how the "little guys" survived. They obviously paid attention to the mental part of the sport.

My doctoral degree in psychology prompted me to look at not only the athlete's body, but the mind as well. The fact was, my body could no longer handle football, and I was too old to get beaten to tar. I wanted to also study a way to improve my own golf game, so I began following the principles that I have now developed into Golf Psyche.

All athletes strive to enter the zone, a peak state of performance called flow, where everything comes easily. In this state, they allow their sense of touch and feel to steer them. They do not have to strain or look for perfection. They just trust what they are doing will work — and they know it will.

When your body and mind work cooperatively and respectfully, golf can be really enjoyable, and even easy (provided you already have the physical skills). Golf is less complicated when you're in the Golf Zone, a kind of trance, or peak performance state, not thinking about if you can play golf or hit a particular shot — you just know you can!

Being in the Golf Zone is when you are able to play golf without thinking too hard — in other words, the game is easy. You are able to take in all the factors of weather, distance, club selection, and importance of the shot, to make a well-thought-out shot. Whether you are winning and planning your celebration, or losing with five holes left, Golf Psyche will keep your mind on the present, to make one shot at a time, and to utilize the Golf Zone for peak performance. But the beauty of Golf Psyche is that you are

conditioned to perform, and do it without negative self-talk
or questions.

The Golf Psyche process will show you how to develop
a structured routine to condition yourself in developing the
optimal mental state, so you can enter the Golf Zone on
demand. It will also teach you how to rebound quickly in
those times when you are playing below your potential or
making mistakes.

The Golf Zone consists of two mental stages, the
Success State and the Focus State.

The first stage, the Success State, is a more conscious
state of mind in which the golfer is interacting with the
environment and operating consciously. The Success State
actually begins on the practice range, but it will be fully
engaged as you begin the first hole. The purpose of the
Success State is to enable you to move in and out of the
Focus State. In the Success State, you will be totally
conscious of all of the following, and enjoy the benefits.

- Sense of calm
- Sense of focus
- Sense of purpose
- Sense of confidence
- Sense of self-trust
- Sense of being successful
- Sense of balance
- Sense of concentration
- Sense of relaxation
- Sense of emotional and physical preparation

The Focus State is the unconscious state, where you move
from interacting with others to a state of complete focus and

concentration. This occurs as you are over the ball and includes the period of time taken for the back swing, hitting the ball, and the follow-through. All these motions are the result of the unconscious mind following the request of the conscious mind. For example, to sink a 20-foot putt, the conscious mind points the direction, detects the break, and takes a few practice swings to get the feel, and the unconscious mind actually determines how hard to hit the ball. When in the Focus State, your mind and body become totally aligned. By following a well-thought-out and conditioned pre-shot routine and utilizing all the teachings of Golf Psyche, you will drop into the Focus State, which will allow your conscious mind to get out of the way and your unconscious mind to make the shot.

Because of the focus of this state, it would be impossible to maintain such concentration for the 4-5 hours it takes to play a round. This is why Golf Psyche defines the Golf Zone as having two parts, the Success State (conscious), and the Focus State (unconscious).

Once the shot is completed, you automatically slip back into the Success State. You may notice that some of the pros on the tour between shots, like Lee Trevino, are very entertaining and appear by times distracted from their game. Trevino can be joking and relaxed, but when he gets over a ball, he slips into a state that allows him to make the shot he wants. All golfers need to know how to allow their minds to relax between shots.

Most golfers find their game is off when the perceived stakes are high and there is an opportunity to create internal pressure and self-doubt. This self-doubt is the beginning of the end for many golfers. Because self-doubt starts with a conscious thought, Golf Psyche is designed to help you develop the conditioning to quiet your conscious mind, eliminating self-doubt and allowing your unconscious mind to guide you to golf success.

Golf Psyche utilizes the most advanced techniques available to enhance your performance. It is important to point out that many of us, in our minds, are pros on the practice range, or in non-tournament play. Both amateurs and pros know that as the stakes rise, so does the internal pressure, and many find it hard to play at their best. The reason this happens is that, as the level of stress increases, conscious mental activity also increases and gets in the way of skill performance.

Golf Psyche has been designed to condition the mind so a golfer needs only to follow the program and learn to trust the unconscious mind. This enables golfers to develop a well-conditioned swing program and be able to use it automatically.

Whether playing for a buck or a million dollars, a player's unconscious mind detects only what the conscious mind sends to it. Golfers who are not conditioned to stay in a peak performance state fall victim to the stress of the conscious mind and experience a drop in performance.

Golf Psyche will teach you to utilize maximum psychomotor (golf skills) potential without allowing the conscious mind to decrease overall athletic performance. Maximum psychomotor skill level can be understood by observing the amount of skill you already have to hit the ball accurately and get good distance. Many golfers can hit good shots, but they are not consistent. Many amateurs remain at that level because they never learn how to develop the mental fitness to play the game to their physical potential.

Success practice formula

As I coach athletes on mental and physical performance, I promote what I call the 40-40-20 success practice formula for conditioning mind and body. It has proven to be powerful and can be adapted to most sports.

The basic premise of this formula is that athletes need to spend their preparation time maximizing their development to help achieve their desired levels of success. The concept is based on a breakdown of time, with 40 percent dedicated to focusing on learning skills, sports psychology, watching self, mental preparation, and coaching; 40 percent, practicing the skills of the sport; and 20 percent, developing body strength and conditioning for the specific sport (e.g., weight training). This formula will be different for each sport, but I have broken it down to make it applicable to golf.

The majority of us have spent about 80 percent of our practice on long shots. With the exception of a small percentage of amateurs, and perhaps a few more professionals, most golfers ignore the mental component of the game.

Many golfers can only measure their results by how a shot looks, or how it felt when they hit the ball. With Golf Psyche, you can develop a mental routine to augment focus and confidence; learn how to be relaxed and calm, and how to let your conscious mind allow your unconscious mind to

Golf Psyche Success Practice Formula

40% of practice time on mental activities	• Mental coaching • Using a program such as Golf Psyche • Learning about golf • Watching a video of yourself • Watching a video of others	• Golf lessons to address the technical aspects of the game • Activities that reduce stress and anxiety • Focus on balancing life
40% of practice time on short irons, 7-iron to putter	• Great emphasis on putting game • Chipping • Wedge • Sand shots	• Focus on short iron excellence • Become great within 100 yards • Develop an effective swing
20% of practice time on 6-iron to driver	• Developing accuracy • Developing power • Developing ability to shape ball (draw or fade)	• Develop consistency • Develop trust • Develop a smooth swing

Golfer A	Golfer B
Can hit the ball well with long irons and is long with his driver (270 yards); is in great physical shape — so let's give him 18/20 for long irons	Straight and relatively short with his driver (220 yards); short, but good accuracy with long irons — Let's give him 15/20, because we are comparing him to Golfer A.
Can't chip very well, and usually 3 putts — let's give him 15/40	Excellent within 100 yards of the green, a bull's eye putter — let's give him this excellent score 34/40
Lacks mental confidence; when he misses one shot, it throws him for the entire round; a real joy to play with; has a temper; but because we still like him, we will give him 15/40.	Great attitude; focused; concentrates well; does not get upset with mistakes; believes in his golf swing; and plays one shot at a time — 35/40
Total score % = 48/100	**Total score % = 84/100**

play golf; and to better determine your present success levels.

The science of this formula can be greatly simplified partially from a common golf adage, "Drive for show and putt for dough." For example, in the chart below, compare the two golfers; observe their percentage breakdown for each area; and you be the judge as to who will be more successful. Which of these two golfers would you want to be?

Golf Psyche has been designed to assist you to improve your entire game. As you look at the analogy of the two golfers, reflect for a moment and

My Percentage Breakdown	
Mental practice	40
Short iron	40
Long iron	20
Total	100

evaluate how your practice breaks down by percentage.

Once you understand and see the value of this formula, you will be able to better understand the power of mental development for peak performance.

Extensive research can be used to confirm the success formula. It clearly points out how important a mental coach is to an athlete's performance, and why many top athletes have their own mental and physical coaches to help them to be top performers.

The position of Golf Psyche is that as long as you have an undamaged nervous system and the psychomotor (technical) skills to perform the physical task of hitting the desired shot (i.e., calling upon all the hundreds of thousands of muscle fibers to move in unison to create the coordination, balance, and strength to hit a golf ball), you should, in theory, be able to replicate the movement at will, regardless of outside stressors.

In the last 100 years, golfers have enjoyed a huge increase in golf technology, but the mental development of the golfer is still far behind the improvements in equipment.

The modern day trend is to purchase the best clubs and balls available, but while today's equipment is far superior to that available 50, or even 5 years ago, and golfers have enjoyed a period of technical advancement over that time, not many of them have made much gain in improving their mental game. In fact, many are not fully aware of their true mental power, although some are now seeing the value of mental coaching.

I see all kinds of folks go out and spend thousands of dollars on equipment, so when I think of the scores that Ben Hogan put up, and the equipment he used, it is quite

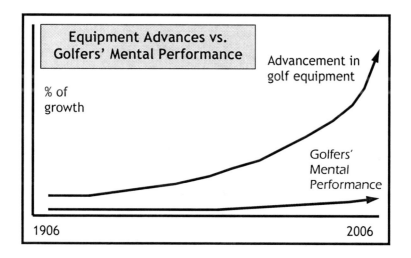

remarkable. He recorded scores similar to today's pros with all their modern gear. It is obvious that Hogan was well prepared mentally and confident on the links. Although I'm sure he would enjoy the benefits of today's clubs and balls, one would only be able to guess at how much better he would be able to dissect a course if he were playing today.

Golf Psyche is like the new equipment of golf. If used correctly, it will improve your game, no matter what your skill level. What stops many from becoming good amateurs, or even turning professional, is not their physical skills, but their mental play. In Golf Psyche, I have developed three extra "clubs" (the *Planning Club*, *Foundation Club*, and *Success Club*) that I am sure the PGA tour will allow you to have. Each of the three Golf Psyche clubs represents the different skills that you can use to improve your game.

The *Planning Club* will help you make a plan and create your desired direction and goals for success on the golf course. To be a good golfer, you need to first have a plan, then take action. The *Foundation Club* is based on allowing you to have the knowledge and skills that enable you to stay in the effective Success State and maintain conscious balance. The *Success Club* will train your unconscious mind to develop the success and muscle memory to perform in golf and to help educate your conscious mind to relax and stay out of the way of your unconscious mind.

If you are performing at 100 percent, playing golf to your full potential on every occasion, you probably won't be needing Golf Psyche, because you're already in your own Golf Zone and everything is perfect, or close to it. Unfortunately, for most of us, this is not the case. The reality is that

99.9 percent of golfers can learn more about how to improve the mental part of their game. Developing the necessary mental focus to learn how to condition the Golf Zone is the main objective of Golf Psyche, so that you can continue to use all the psychomotor skills of playing golf to your maximum physical potential without mental breakdown.

It is important to remember that to develop the mental aspect of the game takes the same discipline and practice as it does to develop the physical part of the game. Golf Psyche is designed to become a part of your routine for golf excellence. As anything in life, this program takes work, a commitment, and effort, although in a short time you will see its benefit. It will be like having your own personal performance golf coach and will be a great guide to personal golf excellence and performance.

In summary, the journey you are going to make is to learn to utilize the power of your mind. You do not need to have any degrees or to be a psychologist to use this program. What you need are a desire, commitment, and the discipline to choose to be a better golfer. As with any journey, it will start off rather slowly, but if you pay attention to the process, before you know it, you will speed up, and you will be enjoying success on the golf course. The real reward will be having the knowledge to succeed.

Golf Psyche Ground Rules

The following Golf Psyche Ground Rules will ensure you are clear about what is important for all golfers to be in touch with.

1. **Identify your physical golf potential.** Some golfers, regardless of the mental preparation and prudent work habits, lack the natural talent and may never be a scratch handicap. So accept the fact that you may never make the PGA tour, but learn to have fun being the best golfer you can be.

2. **Set realistic goals.** A 20-handicap golfer cannot expect, even after Golf Psyche, to become a scratch golfer immediately. Golf Psyche will help you reach your potential by understanding good mental preparation and cutting down on mental error and frustration, but there is no promise that you will become a scratch handicap.

3. **Be clear about the reasons why you play golf.** Do you play for fun? For recreation? To make money? Know the outcome that you want, the kind of golfer you want to be, and the level at which you want to compete.

4. **Make a commitment to the mental process of Golf Psyche.** Understand that to change your thinking is not a one-time event, it is a process. It takes time for cement to dry, it takes time for things to change. Follow the course of Golf Psyche; follow the discipline; and then reap the benefits.

5. **Understand that Golf Psyche is not just about golf.** Utilization of the skills and knowledge that Golf Psyche has to offer will assist other areas of your life. The golfer and the person need to be one; joining the two in harmony will allow you to lead a more peaceful life.

6. **Understand that Golf Psyche is not just a state of mind.** It will also become a state of living, assisting you to become the best you can be in your everyday life.

Planning Club

THE core of Golf Psyche has been designed as a three-phase process (using the metaphor of the three clubs), with each step building on the other, just as you would first use a driver, then an iron, and finally a putter to play a 390-yard, par-4 hole. Each phase represents one of the Golf Psyche clubs. The first two phases are intended to get you close; the third is the "putter" that will make your game a success.

The program is laid out so that chapters 2, 3, and 4 each represent and explain one of the three clubs. The true power of Golf Psyche will be evident when you have the Success Club fully integrated into your daily practice, in relationship to the other two clubs. You will play better and be able to utilize the power of the Golf Zone.

In anything we learn, including golf, there are four stages to mastering a skill:

1. *Unconscious incompetence,* e.g., never knowing anything about Golf Psyche.

2. *Conscious incompetence,* e.g., heard of Golf Psyche, not sure how to do it.

3. *Conscious competence,* e.g., work hard, and can understand Golf Psyche.

4. *Unconscious competence,* e.g., do not need to think about it — Golf Psyche is a part of golf game.

As you move through learning Golf Psyche, you will go from having no concept of the program to the fourth stage of competence, which is unconscious competence. To show and prove you are able to accomplish this, think back to the analogy of swinging a golf club, in which you realized you turned the process over to your unconscious mind that directed your body to make the swing.

Phase One — The Planning Club

The purpose of this phase is to put together an organized and well-thought-out plan of action to improve your golf success. The first thing is to set a clear picture of what you want, then decide what you are willing to do to make this picture a reality. It is important to assess your motivation to want to take the learnings of Golf Psyche and put them into action.

When we are not ready or prepared to improve our golf game and mental preparation (even though we have identified this as a defect), no matter what is done, or no matter what we do, we will not improve our overall game. If we are not motivated to focus on mental preparation, we are choosing to sentence ourselves to remaining exactly where we are. To address this issue, the frame of reference stated below will assist you in your readiness for change, as well as provide a model to help you assess if you are ready to make the personal changes needed to focus on improving your game.

I define personal change as: when a person chooses to want to learn new behaviours that will help the person to be in better control of their life. Psychologists Prochaska, DiClemente and Norcross have developed a six-stage model to assess an individual's motivation for change. I have chosen to use the first four, which are as follows:

Stage 1. *Precontemplation.* In this stage, there is unwillingness to change. Persons in this stage are not psychologically ready or motivated to address improving their mental preparation.

Stage 2. *Contemplation.* In this stage, there is exploration of change. Persons in this stage start to make inquiries and begin to explore the "what ifs" and the potential for change, possibly by improving their mental preparation.

Stage 3. *Preparation.* In this stage, there is concentration and focus on making the change (e.g., reading this program).

Stage 4. *Action.* In this stage, persons are at the point where they are highly motivated to set a specific goal to improve their game. They are ready to take action and carry out the necessary tasks needed to take control of their lives.

For Golf Psyche to be effective, you need to be in the Action stage.

Where have you been, and where are you going?

To get anywhere in life, you need a plan. This phase is intended to allow you the opportunity to make a solid plan and direction. It is really hard getting somewhere if you don't know where somewhere is, or what to do to get there. Too many people forget the importance of making a plan.

Brian Tracy, the popular personal achievement guru, teaches that around 90 percent of all adults never write out a plan, set goals, and monitor them. The purpose of goal setting is to set criteria of what you want and be able to evaluate at any time if you are getting close to your goal. If not, you will need to make adjustments. The most successful performers in the world got there through making a success plan and following it, attaining their short- and long-term goals. A plan will create the environment for conditioning. Through conditioning, we are able to turn beliefs into good habits, which we need for ultimate results.

The goal of Golf Psyche is to assist you to improve your golf game. To do this will take effort, balance, discipline, focus, and determination. If you do not have the motivation and enthusiasm to be specific about what you want, the chances of success will be greatly reduced. You can't fake success; you make it.

Natural laws of golf

Due to natural laws of attraction, what we focus on for the long term will determine what we will get, so if we focus on negative thoughts, the result will be unsatisfactory performance. To become a peak performer, you will need to have a master plan. Tracy says that all of us can become the best that we want. He teaches what he calls natural laws, which he believes are the foundation that supports human beings for making goals and plans.

Law of Control. Be positive about your entire game. The first step is to believe you be positive and can control all parts of your game. It's important that you think about this daily and have positive thoughts.

Law of Cause and Effect. Whenever you miss a shot, understand that mistakes happen and that you are always going to take full responsibility. Someone who gets angry and throws a club is putting the club at cause and themselves at effect. To be a peak performer, you have to accept that what has happened has happened. Though you are the cause of a missed shot, it does not mean you are a failure. Look for the lesson, not the blame.

Law of Beliefs. Whatever your belief about your golf potential and how you continue to hold this belief with emotion, day in and day out, will become true through daily effort.

Law of Expectation. What you believe with confidence will become your self-fulfilling prophecy.

Law of Attraction. Whatever consistent thoughts you have will directly affect the type of situation and people you will have in your life.

The Law of Correspondence. Whatever is happening inside your mind will match the reality of the outside world. Perception of positive internal thoughts and success will present itself on the outside world.

As you consider the above laws, understand that they are laws, not just thoughts. As with the law of gravity, they cannot be changed; they are a part of our world. If you adhere to these laws, you will truly see the benefit of Golf Psyche.

Major golf goal desired

The purpose of this section is not only to help you focus on your golf game, but also to get your entire life balanced. If your relationships are not healthy, no matter what program you follow, you will not achieve your full potential. When setting goals, look at the big picture and consider all the parts. Here are some key points to keep in mind:

- *Specific.* Goals should be detailed as to exactly what they look like, sound like, and feel like, so that if you explained them to someone, you could paint a clear picture.

- *Time limited.* Goals should have time limits that are attainable and can be used as stepping stones for success.

- *Measurable.* Goals need to be observable and measurable by a third party.

- *Checks and balances.* State the consequences of not achieving a goal and the rewards of attaining it. Be clear and specific.

- *High character ethics.* All plans and goals need to be well thought out and of high ethical standards, meaning that nobody will be affected in an inappropriate manner if you obtain your goals.

Exploring personal values

We need to be careful of what and how we perceive ourselves. We can create labels in our minds and project onto ourselves or another person, hence taking on the deficit. To avoid this, we must become aware of our own beliefs and values.

People explore goals, however, few realize that what motivates personal goals is our values. Values are displayed by our personal beliefs. Many people set life goals, but then never check to see how what they want is in direct conflict with their personal value system.

Golf improvement plan

One of the biggest factors about personal growth is to ensure that the road map of what and how you are going to change is clear, and that you fully understand the steps of your golf improvement plan. Realize this plan is designed for you, for what you want for yourself now. You can always update it or make a new one. Take small steps for long-term success. In this section, you have a chance to refine and redefine your goals and plan of action for golf success, having a long-term plan in mind (e.g., to break 80 or 70).

The purpose of a golf improvement plan is to allow you to identify all your desired improvements in the area of golf. It should have one rule: always learn to become a better golfer, but never at the expense of others.

Golf Improvement Plan		
Long-Term Goals	Short-Term Goals	How to Reach My Long-Term Goal
Primary Goal		
	1. _____ 2. _____ 3. _____	_____ _____ _____
Secondary Goal		
	1. _____ 2. _____ 3. _____	_____ _____ _____
Future Goals		
1._____ 2._____	1. _____ 2. _____	_____ _____

Foundation Club

HE Foundation Club is built on six Foundation Pillars: Understanding Human Behaviour; Developing Cognitive Control; The Power of Pre-Supposition; Body Balance; Technically Sound; and Pre-Shot Routine and Master Game Plan.

To be a mentally effective golfer and the most effective golfer you can be, you must first have a solid foundation, both mentally and physically. The following pillars speak to what all golfers who want to be successful have control over. They will be of great value in stabilizing you to set up your conscious mind for positive thought and to allow the process of the Golf Zone to occur naturally. As well, they will help you to create and maintain a vision of the future.

Pillar One — Understanding human behaviour

You have various needs that motivate you to be a good golfer. You may golf because of the need for self-recognition, or the need for self-acceptance. In addition, you may golf because of the relationships you develop on and off the course, the fun, or the freedom that golf gives you.

Dr. William Glasser promotes the basic premise that all human beings have five genetic needs that drive all behaviour. He teaches that all behaviour is purposeful and is intended to meet one or more of these needs. Golf usually meets one or all of the needs: love and belonging, self-worth, self-power, fun, and freedom. Not many people golf for survival, but that also could be one of the driving forces behind your game.

We all develop our own unique individual pictures of what we want as a golfer and how good we want to be. The important component of this section is that when we are on the golf course and hit a shot that we do not like, we may feel a burst of pain that signals the difference between what we want and what we have. To succeed in golf, we need to learn how to take control of ourselves.

For example, most golfers have experienced the frustration of, "%&*($#@), it's in the woods. Why me?" As soon as you experience this frustration, it is important to understand that you, and all golfers, have no alternative but to behave. How you choose to behave will determine how mentally prepared you are. As Glasser teaches, you may not consciously choose to make a specific mistake (to go into the woods), but how you respond is fully your responsibility. The point is, you are always in control of how you behave on a golf course.

Dr. Daniel Goleman, a popular Harvard psychologist, states that people with well-developed emotional skills, referred to as Emotional Intelligence, are more likely to be content and effective in their lives, mastering the habits of mind that foster their own productivity. One key to golf success is being able to keep your composure. Goleman says monitoring our emotions is a key to developing our emotional intelligence.

In a very real sense, we have two minds on the golf course — one that thinks the shot out, and one that keeps us calm so we can make the shot. The thinking mind is the one we are typically conscious of: more prominent in awareness, thoughtful, able to ponder and reflect.

Goleman maintains that the emotional mind is far quicker than the thinking mind, springing into action without pausing for a moment to consider what it is doing. Actions that originate from the emotional mind carry a particularly strong sense of certainty, a by-product of a simplified way of looking at things that can be perplexing to the thinking mind. For example, you lose it because you just missed a shot. When the dust settles, you may find yourself thinking, *What did I do that for?*

Goleman believes this is a sign that the thinking mind has caught up to the incident. Because it takes the thinking mind a moment or two longer to register and respond than does the emotional mind, the first impulse in an emotional situation is the heart's, not the head's. As a golfer, it is important to be aware of this quickness, in which emotions can overtake us before we are even aware they have started. It is essential to be able to control our conscious thoughts. As Glasser teaches, we have control over our reactions. If we let our feelings rule, we will allow for a decreased performance state to be present.

Think back to the last time that you were really upset playing golf. It is a reaction in the brain that causes such outbursts, and it is such moments of impassioned action that we later regret. Once the dust has settled, we wonder how we became so irrational so fast — over a game of golf!

Whenever you hit a shot that creates a difference between what you want (the fairway) and what you have (the woods), you have no choice but to behave (e.g., throw a club, stay calm, etc.). We have to understand that any and all behaviour is an attempt to adjust to the fact that the more desired picture of being on the fairway did not happen. When we get the *want* pictures, the original needs (e.g., self-worth and power) are met. When we throw a club or create internal negative self-talk, we believe at that moment that we have no other choice, so we act out of frustration because our picture was not satisfied.

Ask yourself, does the behaviour of throwing a club help for long-term growth? Of course not! It only provides brief relief, if any at all. The downside, from a Golf Psyche perspective, is that it can upset your psychological domain to the point where you cannot recover. At that point, your

---

Tips to Help Develop Emotional Intelligence

- Be aware of the differences between goals and expectations. You can make a goal of shooting a great round, but if ruled by expectations and those don't occur, you put undue emotional stress onto your system.

- Understand that competition is healthy, but war is a maker of casualties. Play golf with a desire to win, but if you are not on the winning side, prepare your emotional mind not to fight with itself or with others.

- Live your life and play golf with confidence and self-acceptance. Think about living your life without being ruled by hope and fear (e.g., I hope I play well, and so I can keep my card). Hope and fear create negative emotion and stress the emotional brain. Play golf with the intent of pure thought, compassion, and a vision of good. Trust that it will happen!

body is flooded with unnecessary chemicals and you will find it difficult to feel successful or to perform at a level that is within your ability.

Cost of losing your composure

Once we allow ourselves to be caught in the loop of negativity, the whole round of golf is affected, because the consistently negative thinking keeps negative emotion present and facilitates physiological chemical dumping. The body is in a *fight-or-flight* phase and is lacking the fine motor control to perform at its full potential.

Pillar Two — Developing cognitive control

As a golfer, you need to accept and learn that you are a fallible human being (not perfect, and never will be), and you will make mistakes. All of us would prefer not to put the ball into the woods, but if we do, while it is disappointing, it is never totally awful. Losing a child is totally awful; losing a golf ball is not. You'd like to perform better and not go into the woods, but it does not mean that you're not a good person, or not a great golfer. What it means is you went into the woods with your shot and need to find your ball or play another.

Golf is won by the person who makes the fewest mistakes. Please pay close attention to the above wording — *fewest mistakes.* This means that if you are going to play golf, mistakes will happen. The trick is to learn how to reduce their number.

As a golfer, you know that a golf tournament is rarely lost on a single bad shot. Tournaments are usually lost with multiple bad shots due to conscious turmoil. In my opinion, they are lost due to negative thought processes which affect the golfer's performance. We have seen players lose a couple of balls and fall behind, and then recover completely to win a tournament. Why? Because they accepted their circumstances and left the bad shots in the past. They believed they could be successful and maintained pure positive thought. A great golfer is one who has learned to play one shot at a time. When we make a mistake in golf, we need to dispute our less effective thinking and learn how to challenge our negative thoughts. Golf is always played in the present, never in the future or past, although if our heads are in the past or the future, there will be a negative effect on the present.

One of the biggest things I notice in golfers is how they respond to their frustration following a bad shot. The great ones challenge any of their negative self-talk about always being perfect. The best golfers have what world-renowned psychologist Dr. Albert Ellis calls "High Frustration Tolerance." When they perceive frustration, they quickly get rid of it. They remain calm, relaxed, and composed, still believing in their potential and in their ability to get the shot back.

The way your brain works on the golf course is the same way it will think in the real world. You don't have a golf brain and a daily life brain, although some of us may think we do. As you learn to become more positive mentally, be aware of your language. Many people use phrases like "I am terrible, I suck." All of these thoughts, whether internal or expressed, have a negative emotion tied to them. You have the learnings from Glasser and Goleman as to what the physiological costs are for negative emotions and the insight as to what the power of consciousness will dictate. The only way to use this power is through the awareness of continuous positive thought.

We need to prevent negative emotions from ruling us personally and on the golf course. The world has much too much negativity. For you to ever succeed at anything, you need to change your negative talk from "I'm terrible," to "I'll make the next one." Be careful, and do not allow yourself to be ruled by negative emotions. We need to understand how to control our thinking, not only on the course, but in our lives. It is important to learn how to calm the conscious mind so it will not negatively influence the unconscious mind.

Overcoming frustrations

To overcome personal frustrations, we must first recognize and be clear about what is stressful to us (who, what, where, and when). What we are feeling; what our thoughts are; and how our body feels all are important in identifying the origin of frustration, so we can overcome it. Ellis explains that too many people create faulty thinking by making unrealistic rules (e.g., *I should have made that 40-foot putt*). These rules and the use of language like should, must, ought are the reasons that golfers' belief systems get set up for frustration. To help you identify your frustration, answer the following questions.

Pick one frustrating event for this section. You can copy the template on the next page and use it to resolve any of your golf frustrations.

Many times we become more angry when we have set high expectations for our golf success. The high expectation

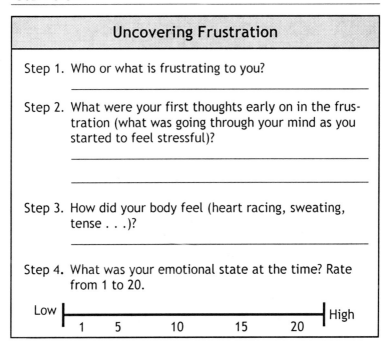

Uncovering Frustration

Step 1. Who or what is frustrating to you?

_____

Step 2. What were your first thoughts early on in the frustration (what was going through your mind as you started to feel stressful)?

_____

_____

Step 3. How did your body feel (heart racing, sweating, tense . . .)?

_____

Step 4. What was your emotional state at the time? Rate from 1 to 20.

Low ⊢————————————————————⊣ High
    1   5   10   15   20

creates unnecessary pressure. To be really good at golf, trust what you do daily to improve. Set realistic goals and work to obtain your best results. Understand that all we can ever do is our best — and the best usually comes naturally and easily from hard work and pure thought. Playing the game should be the fun part and just an extension of great preparation.

Pillar Three — The power of pre-supposition

To assist you in understanding the power of thought, consider the following statement: "Don't think about putting the ball into the woods." — Repeat — Repeat. Now, you probably did not think about going into the woods! The truth is, though, that many of you did, in fact, think about putting the ball into the woods. Right? Wow! How did that happen? It's called pre-supposition. Pre-suppositions are the internal pictures we frequently, and inadvertently, create in our heads.

To see the power of pre-supposition, consider when you have said to yourself, *Don't go into the woods,* your mind must create the negative picture of going into the woods to fully understand the statement. Our brains cannot accept a negative, thus the brain drops the "don't," and follows the instruction, "go into the woods." To overcome this, you must practice *Outcome Based Pre-suppositions.* Every time you play out a golf shot, program your thinking to allow yourself to think only what you want to happen. Our minds are much in tune with what we want, so you will need to be clear. Be a pro and say where you want to go with each and every shot! So think success! In your pre-shot routine, we will review when and how to use pre-supposition. It is really important to be mindful of what you are saying about what you want. This is another important way to avoid negative emotions.

Pillar Four — Body balance

Now that you have been introduced to human behaviour; how to eliminate and/or limit self-destructive thinking; and to pre-supposition, it is appropriate to introduce the fourth pillar of the Foundation Club: daily exercise, rest, diet, and relaxation.

The foundation of all health is based on diet, exercise, rest, and relaxation. We all need to be aware of what we are feeding ourselves, as well as how we are treating ourselves. But before you start any major health change, please see your doctor for approval.

No matter what you do in regard to playing golf, for example, using the best equipment, having coaches both for your physical and mental game, there is one law you can never ignore that will always determine if you will be a great golfer or not. It is the natural law of health. Unless you have your health (physical and mental), you cannot succeed for the long term.

If you develop an illness or have a sports injury, the only way to get your game on track is to understand that how you choose to respond to your concern will have a direct relationship to how quickly you will get your health back, or maintain it.

If you drive a car without oil for 200 miles, what happens? If you drive your unhealthy body, what happens? That's right, it breaks down!

To achieve golf excellence, you need to achieve personal health. If you have a poor diet and sleep habits, drink too much, have no mental coach, no golf coach, play with average gear, and have a negative belief about the importance of health — and still shoot 72 consistently . . . Congratulations!

My question is, what could you really do if you focused more on health? Would your game improve or get worse?

Golf Psyche believes we need to respect our bodies like our equipment. I rarely see a golfer abuse his new clubs, but you will see golfers chip away at their health by not respecting it. It too often takes a health crisis or significant scare to motivate people to make healthy choices.

One suggestion: before you do anything, just ask yourself, *is this going to help me for the long term, or is it just a short-term quick fix?* Those who keep their course for the long term are rarely just lucky to have their health — they have earned it!

Designing a healthful eating lifestyle

Follow your body; listen carefully to what foods make you feel good and what foods do not. Ask yourself before you eat any food, "Does my body really want this?" The best approach is self-awareness, because our bodies all have individual needs and no one diet is right for everybody. Eating small portions (e.g., 4-5 small meals), especially breakfast, is a good way to remain physically and psychologically healthy. One of the best rules is to eat when you are hungry, not because you think you need to. If you need to learn about healthy eating, see your local fitness folks. They will be more than helpful. Monitor your intake of fat, caffeine, and alcohol, to regulate the nutritional value of your diet, and drink as much good water as you can.

Exercise

Exercise is essential to maintaining a healthy lifestyle. Exercise does not mean only fitness centres, it means doing something that moves the muscles and increases the heart rate. I recommend getting your heart rate up to 185, minus your age, for a minimum of 20 minutes, three to four times a week. If you are unable to attend a fitness centre, going for a brisk walk is an excellent way to increase your heart rate and reduce stress. I personally believe strength training is important for all golfers, and I highly recommend it.

Rest

The average adult requires 6 to 8 hours of sleep. Rest is also essential in maintaining a healthy lifestyle. The best source of rest is to develop healthy sleep patterns that reduce the effects of daily stress, and allow the body to recuperate and prepare itself for the next day's stresses. Disturbed sleep in itself can be stressful. Learning to relax will be of value for healthy sleep.

To be healthy, it is important to schedule time to rest and take care of your body. Everyone has a different amount of needed sleep time. The key to figuring out how much you need is to monitor how you feel when you wake up in the morning.

Time management for promoting relaxation

The key to relaxation is making the time in your day to do it — every day. Make to-do lists and prioritize the items on them. This allows you to separate important jobs from the many time-consuming trivial ones and gives you control of the serious challenges. To-do lists are extremely useful for organization and for motivating yourself to achieve what you want to accomplish.

Relaxation

The Success Club will be a relaxing process. However, above and beyond this process, I strongly promote the importance of developing a couple of relaxation techniques that help you return to a calm state. You already know the cost of losing emotional control, and how your body's physiology pays the price. The purpose of good daily relaxation is to educate your body to know how to stay calm. One key to golf success is being able to stay relaxed and calm, to stay within oneself.

Pillar Five — Technically sound

To become a great golfer, you will need to ensure you are technically sound, which I define as having developed your own swing and golf skills and feel comfortable with what you are doing. There are many experts in the field whose purpose is to improve the physical part of your game.

Golf Psyche is not a program for teaching you how to play the game technically (e.g., grip, swing, plane, etc.), it is designed to improve the skills you presently have through the development of your thought process. Trust your own instincts and listen to your body. It is helpful when developing the cognitive domain to ensure you also have a focus on skill acquisition ability and are using the appropriate equipment. Golf Psyche is designed to develop the mind and body connection.

To develop your skills for golf, I recommend the following:

- Ensure you are fitted for your clubs by someone who is an expert in personalizing clubs.

- Buy equipment that matches your skill level. It is important that as you improve as a golfer you are using quality equipment. Your local PGA pro will be a good person to talk to about club and ball selection.

- Become a student of the game. Watch and read about what the pros are doing. This is invaluable, because it will provide you with data to choose from when you are practicing and playing the game.

- Work with your golf teacher and a mental coach to help you determine the tempo of game and swing that fits your physical potential, personality, and mental concentration.

- Get golf lessons from a PGA pro or certified golf coach. You will be amazed at how much your game will improve by having a professional watch your swing and provide instant feedback. The pro will provide you with homework to take to the practice range.

- Practice. The key to being technically sound is to incorporate a well-thought-out practice routine, following the 40-40-20 success practice guidelines. The technical part of the game Golf Psyche will concern itself with is the pre-shot routine.

Pillar Six — Pre-shot routine & master game plan

In Phase Three (Success Club), we will be working on a structured process to teach you how to enter the Focus State, where you are able to have complete and total concentration on hitting the ball where you want it to go, and being in a flow state, where you are relaxed, calm, and comfortable. The key to golf performance excellence is the ability to maintain your concentration, while understanding that it is impossible to maintain peak concentration for 4 or 5 hours, the time it takes to play a round of golf.

To be effective on the course, you will need a pre-shot routine, which is a set procedure that you follow before every shot. Having an established routine assists in keeping the body in flow and helps you overcome distracting circumstances, such as tournament pressure. Once you have developed a pre-shot routine, before every golf game make a master game plan to decide how you will play each hole on the course.

The purpose of the pre-shot routine is to have a structure in your game that you condition to become automatic. Once it is learned, the routine becomes as automatic as tying your shoelaces (meaning you no longer need to think about it, and you do it the same way every time). The pre-shot routine may take a great deal of practice to be completely automatic, however, monitoring and keeping track of it will assist you to fully incorporate it into your game. So be patient and keep a record of how often you use it, and work to improve your score.

This routine will become the key method of entering and exiting the two parts of the Golf Zone. The pre-shot routine will act as a switch to move from the outside world to back inside your head, and to start the process of tuning in the focus and concentration, to assist your mind and body to connect to allow for flow and to be in the Golf Zone.

You may feel uncomfortable and strange in the early stages of developing your pre-shot routine, but in a short time, when it goes to your unconscious mind and becomes almost always automatic, you will be well aware of its value and importance to your golf success.

Developing Your Pre-Shot Routine

The following guidelines will help you to develop your pre-shot routine and make it easy and effective.

1.   Have a game plan before playing the round. Plan your shot; pick your club; and be aware of the envi-

ronment. All of these processes allow for commu-
nication both inside (e.g., self-talk) and outside
(e.g., talking to caddie or partner).

2. Start the process. The best way to start the pre-shot
routine is to utilize a kinesthetic process in which
you touch something to tune in your mind that you
are about to make a shot, that it is time to start to
move to the Focus State (e.g., tapping your club on
the ground in a particular way in front of you, to
signal the start of the process). This trigger is the
signal for you to shut out the outside world and to
be totally focused inside. What the pros do —
many of them without realizing it — is have the
same habit (touching their hat in the same place
before each shot) that acts as a trigger to be prepared and to get focused. Other examples are grab-
bing their glove, shirt, or pants in the same location
and manner before they approach each shot. It is
important to pick your starting trigger consciously,
until it becomes unconscious.

3. Before taking a perfect practice swing, look at the
target and see the ball go to the specific point. I recommend no more than two true full swings behind
the ball, but develop your own personal preference.
Just be consistent for every shot. Swing as if you
were taking the actual shot at the target. This calls
up the nervous system to prepare the muscle bun-
dles that you will actually need and prepares them
for what you are going to ask them to do. In this
process, once again it is important that when you

swing the club, you see the ball go where you want it to, stating the pre-supposition of the shot with your success affirmation (you will learn this in the Success Club).

4. Release tension. As you move from behind the ball to the setup for the shot, release any residual tension with relaxation breaths that relax you (e.g., two deep, full breaths).

5. Address the ball. Line up your shot and see your target. Whenever you look at a target, no matter how far it is, see in your mind's eye where you are and exactly where you want the ball to go. I teach the **telescope technique**. Imagine the ball attached to the club as you look at a target. As you do this, imagine the club extending like a telescope, to put the ball down in the exact spot you want it to go. I suggest you use this proc-

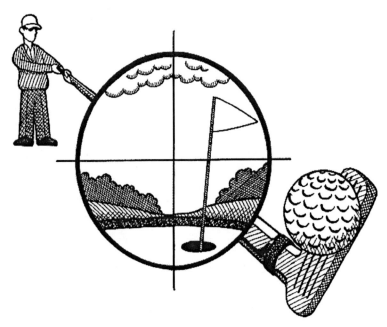

ess for a 2-foot putt or a 200-yard 3-iron. In this stage, you will be on the verge of the deepest part of the Focus State and you will consciously align the ball. The actual swing comes when you are in the Focus State, when your unconscious mind has the needed information and will know how to swing the club. See the target, say a positive affirmation word, such as "smooth," and start to swing the club full. Once you say your word, this is the signal to **PULL THE TRIGGER AND SWING YOUR CLUB.**

Any dialogue or golf strategy should be done behind the ball. By the time you get over the ball, you need to be well into the Focus State. Once you line up the ball and are just about to enter the Focus State, all dialogue has stopped. If it continues, just stop, and start again. If you have a difficult time concentrating, "jam" the negative thoughts with a word which you have planted through repeated practice (e.g., Smooth!), and just repeat the word until the shot is hit successfully. The purpose is to not allow the effects of the Focus State to be influenced by any negative internal dialogue or last-minute corrections.

When designing your pre-shot routine, it is important to remember the law of inertia: Something in motion will move more easily than something stopped. When over the ball, be relaxed and moving slightly. You should stop only for a brief second, so all of your body can move as one during the swing. It is important to use the same micro movements with each shot (e.g., three firm half swings behind the ball). This helps develop a consistent routine.

A few points to consider when you are developing your pre-shot routine: it is best to think of the entire process as if you are winding up a spring, and from start to finish (hitting the ball), your routine should be within the same time frame. If there are any delays, you should start the routine from the top. The purpose of this process is to open the window of opportunity to step into the Focus State. It also will help as pressure increases, because it will distract your conscious mind and help it focus on one shot at a time. A pre-shot routine will be from the trigger to start the process, to hitting the ball — in the range of 10 to 30 seconds. I recommend you have your routine timed and videotaped, so you are aware of its structure and length.

How to develop your pre-shot routine

In the space below, brainstorm all the parts of your pre-shot routine and what you want it to look and feel like.

1. Write a paragraph of what and how you want your entire pre-shot routine, following the guidelines provided.

    _____

    _____

    _____

2. From the above pre-shot routine, using the template on Page 49, define keywords that prompt your process in a logical order. It should be no longer than 5-6 points. Be specific in your mind of how and what it looks like (e.g., wiggle once or three times; be consistent).

My Pre-Shot Routine	
Keyword	What I will be doing
1.	
2.	
3.	
4.	
5.	
6.	

Make a commitment to use this process for every shot, so you will be able to move in and out of the two parts of the Golf Zone. Understand that you may not follow your pre-shot routine every time, because you forget or become distracted.

The pre-shot routine is one major resource for preventing pressure from getting to you too much. All you do is trust your preparation and pass the shot over to your routine, focusing on one shot at a time, trusting your unconscious mind to perform. It is like having a seatbelt on in a car — it keeps you in place and secure in what you are capable of doing.

I believe it is important to prepare consistently, to have a good starting routine, and to stick to it. I have developed a tee off preparation.

Golf Psyche tee off preparation

1. Have your game plan established and written out.

2. Have your pre-shot routine clearly established and follow it.

3. Do the Success Club process 30-60 minutes prior to round. Set your goal for the round.

4. Drink 2-3 glasses of water before tee off and take a bottle of water with you for the round. Drink water generously throughout the round. Have a power snack as well.

5. Ensure that you have followed your normal practice routine.

6. As you stand on the tee box, allow yourself to slip into the Success State, using the peripheral vision activity (explained in Chapter 4).

7. Become aware of only creating positive pre-suppositions and be mindful of how relaxed, smooth, and strong you are.

8. Take a few good deep breaths.

9. Fire off a few positive anchors and release a peak state to convince your conscious mind that you are ready.

10. Use the success affirmation.

11. Have fun, and send out the first shot with success.

Master plan

In addition to having a great and well-planned pre-shot routine, I believe that a master plan is what will enable you to stay on track and follow your pre-shot routine. Before you even get to the course, it is important to create a master plan of how you will play it.

- What is your plan to attack the course?
- What club will you tee off with on No. 2?
- What weather conditions do you need to be able to stick to your plan?
- What is the forecast for the day?

- What score are you planning on, based on your skill level?
- What do you have to be aware of in regard to trouble areas?
- What are the greens speeds?
- What time of day are you playing the round, and what is its effect on the course?
- What are you playing the round for (e.g., fun, tournament, scouting the course)?
- Where is the course information regarding distance and hole design?
- What course knowledge do you have?
- Have you been initiated to the course?
- Have you asked any of the locals how the course is playing?
- Do you know how the course is playing?

These are only a few of the questions you need to answer when preparing to play a course. I suggest that you have the above information collected and organized, so you can make a master plan for your round. All sports spend a great deal of time making well-thought-out game plans, and golf is no different. For the best success, ensure you have a master game plan.

The template on Page 52 will help you become aware of your master plan.

This Master Game Plan provides an overview for a well-planned round of golf. With this preplan, you need only follow your pre-shot routine on the course, utilizing the Success and Focus states, so you can perform in the Golf Zone. The above process is great for you left-brain golfers, because

Master Game Plan

Course name				Weather forecast		Date	

Hole	Par	Tot. Yds	1st Club Yardage	2nd Club Yardage	3rd Club Yardage	Green Speed	Main Hole Points
1							
2							
3							
4							
5							
6							
7							
8							
9							
10							
11							
12							
13							
14							
15							
16							
17							
18							

Game analysis?   Y   N   Comments:

you like organization. It also helps the right-brainers to become focused and organized.

Since golf is a game of variety (e.g., the ball goes into the woods on No. 2), there is a need to be flexible, creative, and intuitive. All situations cannot be preplanned, so understand that you start with a master plan, which will be adjusted many times because of circumstances. For instance, if the weather changes; if you miss a shot; if there is a need to go for a shot to win, you will have to adjust your plan. The master plan provides you with a model and strategy, so understand it is just a plan, and not law. Trust your instincts, and be aware that change may occur, so when in difficulty (e.g., a ball goes into the woods), the master plan can be used to regain your focus and start you off again in the right state.

When conditions settle down, get back to your master plan.

Many golfers will spend the time and will have a well-thought-out game, because they have a desire to advance to the next level of skill. One of the fundamentals for golf success is having a plan of attack and the ability to adjust the plan as needed on the course.

In summary, ensure you are a student of the game and have a plan to learn the technical parts of golf, so you can become the best you can be. Your ability to trust that you can learn, excel, and become successful is also deeply seated through positive thought. I teach athletes to trust their instincts. All of us are individuals; trust what feels good and learn to go with it. Also, never be afraid to get a second opinion about technical questions. Find a golf teacher who will work with your natural talents and who appears interested in you as a person. Golf has too many people who are into their *pride*. Those folks have negative energy and emotion. You need a teacher who operates like Harvey Penick, who teaches because of the joy his students bring him, as well as having an opportunity to share their learnings.

The Foundation Club is an important part of Golf Psyche. It helps educate and prepare the conscious mind to have the knowledge and skills to assist the unconscious mind to perform — and for you to have the awareness of how to manage your emotions, so you can tap into the power of positive emotional consciousness. Golf is largely a mental game — the outcomes will be based on what we do in regard to physical and mental preparation. To be a great golfer, you need to have a solid foundation.

Success Club

I N the Planning Club and Foundation Club, I explained the importance of a solid foundation and of having direction. The more mentally prepared you are, the better the chances of hitting your target: golf success. As in any process, it only works if you work, so be the best you can, and take the necessary steps. The importance of conscious awareness and pure thought will help to catapult you to the next level of performance. This is obtained by living by high principles and healthy living, both physically and mentally.

The Success Club is the stage for conditioning your mind to move from the Success State to the Focus State and to train your unconscious mind to assist your body to perform to its full potential. The first two clubs are intended to have you develop the skills to progress to the Success State and to create a healthy awareness of how to have positive conscious thought. Eventually, you will not differentiate between the two states; they will flow together and you will just be in a Golf Zone, going in and out of the two states without conscious recognition.

This section outlines a structured process that, with practice, will provide you with the mental preparation and concentration to enter the Focus State on demand. In other words, you will enjoy the game of golf because you will have the knowledge and skills to put yourself at the necessary peak state, believing that you can hit the desired shot because you are both mentally and physically prepared.

Success setup

Before we start, it is important that you get prepared and focused for this process. To be successful, we need to believe that what we are doing will be of benefit.

The key is to help you get into the state of wanting to improve and grow, and to tune in your motivation. Sometimes you may need to take a break and come back. The point is that when you choose to follow this process, just going through the motions will not help. You need good form — the same conscious attention to detail as your physical practice of golf.

The purpose here is to get you emotionally, cognitively, and physically prepared. Complete the following checklist so that you are able to obtain the greatest benefit from the Success Club.

Success Club preparation

1. Find a quiet spot and relax.

2. Focus in on your purpose and outcome.

   • How motivated are you to go through this process? To continue, ensure you are close to a 10, on a scale of 0 to 10.

   • What are you doing this process for?

   • What is your belief about your potential?

   • Are you prepared to accept the new and exciting mental development you are going to obtain?

3. Do warm-up breathing. For five minutes, do the following exercise: Breathe in through your nose for 5 seconds, and breathe out through your mouth, making a "Ha" sound, for 10 seconds. This technique is a powerful method of preparing your mind and ensuring you have the correct and necessary oxygen supply.

Four Steps of the Success Club

As an athlete, when you are able to prepare your unconscious mind to allow you to prepare your body to develop the "memory muscle blueprints" of golf excellence, you will enjoy greater success. This section utilizes a process that will assist you to condition your conscious mind to put you in the Success State and to allow your conscious mind to perform in the Focus State. This process is facilitated at a conscious level and trains the unconscious mind.

To get to the highest level, one need not try to force success. Based on the law of attraction, good thoughts, clear pictures of success, a plan, specific goals, and self-discipline will attract success to you.

Step 1 — *Success State preparation:* The following process will help to condition you to move into the Success State any time you walk onto a golf course to play or practice. This will prepare you to move into the Focus State. This procedure comes from the work of Dr. Tad James, who is making revolutionary breakthroughs in human change. This exercise teaches you how to use your peripheral vision versus normal vision. When using peripheral vision, you are able to be in a state that allows for peak performance. It has the effect of a minor self-trance, meaning when you enter it, you are in the state for attaining golf success.

The Success State is facilitated by the golfer concentrating and being in a relaxed, receptive state of mind. Becoming relaxed should be verified by saying to yourself, *That's it. Very good!* Practice the following for two minutes and repeat internally a verification word to indicate relaxation. Do not strain your eyes.

Before each round (or practice), stand on the No. 1 tee, relax, and allow your mind to enter the Success State by doing the following eye exercise. Before you know it, you will be in the Success State and will be able to concentrate

---

Golf Psyche Success State Preparation

1. Put your eyes up and centered, as if to look at the space between the eyebrows. A spot in the clouds or on a wall will do.

2. Closely monitor yourself for the first sign of relaxation and centeredness. You will notice that there are certain signs of relaxation: the rate of respiration will slow down, muscle tension in the face will ease, your eyes will not be blinking as much as usual. It is important to do this for two minutes or less, otherwise eyestrain may result.

3. Verify that you are relaxed, through internal dialogue (e.g., *That's right – very good*).

4. Remain physically and mentally relaxed, and move your eyes down. You are now in the Success State. This will help you to be confident, and by using the power of peripheral vision, to easily and effortlessly increase your performance level.

easily and effortlessly. The procedure to enter this state takes practice, but by doing the following exercise, you will learn how to do it.

I have included this in this section because it is a great activity to practice daily, so you can condition your mind to enter a state that supports peak performance. To be consistent, keep yourself in tune with positive thought. Every time you do this activity, it means the beginning of a new round, and that it's time to enter the Success State.

Step 2 — *Golf Psyche Simulation:* The purpose of this step is to start to condition your mind to Simulation Imagery (using mental imagery to enhance performance). You have already prepared your mind, removed any negative emotions, and are in the Success State. This section is similar to practicing golf, but it is all in your mind. The benefit is that it allows you to practice playing flawless golf, to achieve goals, and to see success, creating the experience of a successful history. This will give you the "I have done this before, so I can do it again" attitude. It starts to program your mind and body, and when you process a complex task like golf in your head, the task becomes easier. Mental concentration develops success. This process will teach your mind to stay focused on the course, and it teaches your body how to relax and stay calm when playing golf. The action of this stage turns the mental imagery into a simulation that can be as valuable as the actual physical practicing, because even though it is mental imagery, it is still teaching the body how to perform the task and will set up your body to blueprint your golf swing by programming memory muscle.

How to begin

As with any exercise, begin slowly. Start with an easy imagery, like a couple of simple holes that are fairly easy, and work up to the more challenging ones. You will be conditioning your mind with your physical abilities. As you begin this exercise, it will become very obvious that it is designed for the visual part of your brain. I have chosen this because the best way to train your mind is visually, but if you have a hard time seeing pictures in your head, you can train the visual part of your brain through practice.

You may think you cannot see pictures in your head, but what is the colour of your golf bag? What is your license plate number? What is your street number? How did you get the answer? Your brain generated images of them — you saw pictures in your head.

It is important to explain that you do not or will not see pictures on the inside as clearly as in the outside world, although through practice you will become very good at seeing clear visual images and colours, and will eventually be able to play an entire round in your head, like a video recording.

Do not be concerned when you practice Golf Psyche simulation imagery for 3-4 weeks, before you really see obvious results. (As with most anything, learning and growth start slowly, and after time and practice you will build up your skills, but by being patient and disciplined, and practicing with conviction, the results will be outstanding.

Golf Psyche Simulation Imagery

This activity will take about 15-20 minutes.

1. Put on some personally soothing music. This will help to integrate the left and right brains for ultimate learning and programming.

2. Using the following visualization warm-up, you will further prepare yourself for golf practice simulation.

    a. Close your eyes.

    b. Pick a fruit (e.g., an orange).

    c. Look at the orange and describe it in detail. On a scale of 1 to 10, how clear is the orange?

    d. Now imagine you are in your kitchen and the orange flies out the window.

    e. Now imagine you are chasing it; see yourself flying after the orange and then catching it.

    f. Bring the orange back to the kitchen, let it go three times, and each time see yourself catch it faster. Now, on the same scale, how clear is the orange? You will notice the number will be higher after the exercise. This is a sign that your visualization performance centre is tuned in. Through practice, it will improve.

    This is a method to tune in your mind for peak performance visualization and conditioning. **Note: Once you get advanced, you can skip Step 2.**

3. Set up your brain for full integration by allowing yourself to go into an accelerated learning state. Research shows that we walk around in what is called a beta state. We can learn in this state,

however, if we relax ourselves into the alpha state, we can triple or quadruple our learning ability, which is important for conditioning the mind. The best way to enter the accelerated learning state is by using autogenetics, a form of self-hypnosis. In this process, follow this routine:

a. Get in a comfortable position

b. Repeat the following statements for each of the left arm, right arm, left leg, right leg, chest, and head.

My _____ is getting heavy and warm — 3 times

My _____ is totally relaxed — 2 times

Within a short period of time, you will have been able to teach your body to relax and prepare for the learning and self-programming that will follow.

4. Now that you are relaxed and comfortable and visualization is easy for you, in your mind's eye, pick the appropriate golf course (one you play regularly or are going to play), and see yourself on No. 1 tee under the best of conditions, playing with your favourite people. See yourself alone in the tee box where it's quiet, the sun is shining, and the wind is whistling gently through the trees. Smell the smells — the magic aroma of freshly cut grass, the fresh air, the evergreens. As you stand there looking towards the magnificent No. 1 hole, say to yourself how excited and proud you are, how happy you are to be there today. First, see yourself doing the Success State eye exercise. Incorporate your pre-shot routine

into each shot (remember to pick a target, using the telescope technique), and feel yourself go into the Focus State each time you make a golf swing. Be aware that you are in the Golf Zone, are able to concentrate, and visually play this hole perfectly, and then go on to play the entire round in your head, one shot at a time. Train yourself to stay in the present and avoid looking at the past or future. Think only of the game at hand and focus on one shot at a time. Avoid the deception of poor form and by thinking of the shortcuts — there are none — only through self-discipline, good form, and positive thought will this procedure succeed. This process will take repeated practice, and the more you practice, the more concentration you will develop. The biggest challenge for many golfers is to develop concentration and to move into a peak performance state at will. Remember as you learn this process to start slow, visually play a few holes, and gradually work up to an entire round.

Have the same routine for each shot and see yourself hitting only shots that are successful; no errors can occur in your simulated round — you're playing great. This exercise will assist you in conditioning the use of positive pre-supposition to support the goal of success. It also is educating your mind and telling your unconscious mind what to do every time.

5. Once you have mastered playing an entire round in your head, you can add the advanced step, called the

---

Golf Psyche Visualization Process

Complete the six steps of the visualization process. *Note: On No. 1 hole, enter the Success State.*

1. Pick the hole you are going to visualize first.
2. See the shot you want to make. I suggest you have a game plan of the shot prepared; have your target picked; and use the telescope technique to be exact in target location.
3. See yourself through your own eyes go through your pre-shot routine.
4. Enter the Focus State, hit the shot, and see it go to your desired target.
5. Anchor the success of your shot, using a kinesthetic anchor.
6. Provide a positive affirmation of your shot and ensure you have positive, pure thoughts.

Golf Win Generator. To do this, you first play your perfect round of golf. Once you have played it, you start to look to a light in the future that's right over the hill. As you look at the future in your image, start to think about all the perfect thinking and dreams you want to happen in golf, such as a game of five under par in an upcoming event. Think about every detail of the game and describe how it will look and feel after you win. See yourself winning and sharing all the conscious positive emotion the victory will create for others and yourself. Be very specific, down to the slightest sounds and visual effects. Through practice, and using the power of imagination and thought, these positive images can help to create a new destiny. This process can be truly powerful, so with practice, concentration, and self-discipline, the reward will be great golf.

I recommend you use the Golf Psyche visualization process in relationship to daily practice for the particular course you are going to play. I also suggest that, once you have your golf plan designed, you play your planned round using this process.

In summary, a great deal of research supports the theory that mental rehearsal has a similar benefit to physical practice. It allows you to practice golf error-free and simplifies the game for the unconscious mind. This exercise helps to allow the conscious mind to develop confidence and to be able to trust the unconscious mind to succeed in the Focus State.

Step 3 — *Conditioning the Success State through anchoring:* Anchoring your body every time you create success is the key to repeated success. Every time you create a positive picture from now on, whether it be doing Simulated Imagery or actually practicing or playing golf, you will benefit from anchoring this peak state of accomplishment.

The purpose of practicing anchors is to get into the habit and develop the ability to fire off an anchor prior to hitting the ball, to set up your conscious mind in a programmed success state. This helps to keep you in the Success State and allows your mind to be ready to perform to its potential upon demand at any time, simply by firing off the desired anchor. After every good shot, you will benefit by anchoring it. This develops a stimulus-response, so that eventually, when you fire your anchor, your mind will remember

Creating Success Anchors

The best way to anchor yourself is to first get into a highly emotional state (e.g., when you are in your self-imagery). Prior to this, identify the positive anchor you are going to use for golf success and confidence.

1. To anchor yourself, think about what you want to anchor. Bring to mind one specific golf success, like making a 40-foot putt. When you feel, see, or hear this success at its peak, set the anchor (e.g., middle knuckle, left middle finger), by touching the anchor for 5-8 seconds, and say your anchoring word (e.g., Smooth!). Once you do this, think of something neutral and then create another long-putt success. Repeat this process 8 to 10 times to really condition the anchor.

2. Now, test your anchor. Fire it off by touching it and saying "Smooth!" If the anchor is in place, you will have a clear picture and feeling of making the long putt. Understand that anchors can also be negative, so be aware of old negative anchors and replace them with new positive ones. Anchoring is a positive tool and takes practice.

Note: In golf, you can create anchors for specific kinds of shots to create, or you can create one universal anchor to put you into a state of confidence.

exactly the state it was in during the last great shot and will set you up for another success so that your conscious mind does not get worried and talk the unconscious mind out of what it can do.

An anchor can be visual, auditory, or kinesthetic (touch). Pick an anchor location and associate it with what you want. For purposes of Golf Psyche, you want to know that you can make the upcoming shot. The anchor provides an ability to instantly enter a confident state of success.

Every time you hit a great shot, either in your mind or on the course, anchor it by saying a word or words and touch the anchor location. Through repetition, you will have conditioned the anchor, so that every time you want to hit a good shot, by touching your anchor, you will activate the Success State, re-experience the calm and satisfaction of hitting the good shot, and setting up your mind for success. When on the practice range, after you hit a good shot, be sure to anchor it.

Anchoring is based on stimulus-response association. The more you do something, the stronger the conditioning. For example, if you like a hockey team, you need only to see the visual picture of just a part of the team to quickly have a good feeling. Positive anchors will do the same thing, although with anchoring you can choose what you want to program into your mind. For example, the science of anchoring is used in the pre-shot routine to indicate the time to move from the Success State into the Focus State.

Anchoring allows us to choose to create, and have, a desired internal state when we want it. You can use whatever you want for an anchor. What you need to do is to be focused and associate the state to the anchor, so that firing the anchor will create the desired state.

When to use anchors? Whenever you want to feel consciously good about an upcoming shot, fire off your anchor and whenever you make a good shot, anchor it. I strongly suggest you incorporate this anchor into your pre-shot routine. If you use more than one anchor, remember what all of them are for, and you may want to record them on your golf plan to ensure 100 percent accuracy.

Step 4 — *Positive success affirmation:* Now that you've come this far, give yourself a hand and recognize your efforts. Whenever you are involved in golf imagery or on the course, give yourself what Dr. Eric Berne calls "positive strokes" for self-acceptance, to build on what we talked about in the Foundation section, Ellis' "unconditional positive acceptance," knowing that no matter how you perform, you are a good person. Making the shot does not affect what you basically are, so a bad shot does not make you a bad person; it just means you are human. A positive stroke for unconditional self-acceptance allows you to condition internal reward, so you can continue having positive pure thought. This means that the only judge, in the end, will always be you, and you will always give yourself acceptance. Remember, golf is a game, and your intent is to do your best. Whatever the outcome, you have had a chance to enjoy the game.

Affirmation to Maintain the Success State

- As you walk up to any shot (e.g., 40 feet from a green), before even starting your pre-shot routine, recognize what you need to do (e.g., 10-foot putt for par).
- Say to yourself your affirmation — *I am a great putter.*
- See yourself make the putt.
- Feel yourself making the putt.
- Relax, release your feeling, and feel proud of how mentally and physically prepared you are. When you are ready, start your pre-shot routine.

This stage is to reward your conscious mind for trusting your unconscious programming. This process is very powerful for creating and setting up a success affirmation and pure positive thought. Whenever you walk between shots, remember you are OK, and use the success affirmation to keep you in the Success State. The method outlined below is another effective way to use success affirmation.

In review, the Success Club will train your conscious mind to be able to further utilize the Success State and the learning of the first two clubs. It will also teach you how to move from the Success State to the Focus State.

To sum up, Golf Psyche has three phases. Within each phase are specific learnings and techniques to improve your mental preparation. Phases One and Two are foundation phases and Phase Three is the action stage. Through vigilance and great focus, the three stages of Golf Psyche will greatly improve your golf game, as well as enhance your sense of well-being.

References

Berne, E. (1972). *What do you say after you say hello.* New York: Graves Press.

DiClemente, C., and Norcross, J. (1992). In search of how people change: Application to addictive behaviors. *American Psychologist, 47,* 1102-1114.

Ellis, A. (1980). *Growth through thought.* Palo Alto, CA: Science and Behavior Books.

Gallwey, W. T. (1998). *The inner game of golf.* New York: Random House Inc.

Glasser, W. (1998). *Choice theory. A new psychology of personal freedom.* New York: Harper & Row.

Goleman, D. (1995). *Emotional intelligence.* New York: Bantam.

James, T. (1997). Master Practitioner Neuro-Linguistic Programming, presented at Advanced Dynamics Neuro-Linguistic Training. Kona, HI.

Penick, H. (1997) *The wisdom of Harvey Penick.* New York: Simon & Schuster.

Robbins, A. (1991). *Awaken the giant within.* New York. Simon & Schuster.

Tracy, B. C. (1997). *Action guide for personal achievement.* Niles, IL: Nightingale Conant.

Appendix

Individual Golf Psyche Activities

Recognizing your personality type

Personality type affects a person's view of the world and stress level, especially how they respond on the golf course. The following will help you recognize your personality features. Circle the number that best represents your own behaviour.

Am relaxed when I miss a shot.	1 2 3 4 5	Upset when I miss a shot.
Am not competitive with peers.	1 2 3 4 5	Am very competitive with peers.
Never feel rushed during the golf round.	1 2 3 4 5	Always in a hurry to get to the next shot.
Solve one golf technical problem at a time.	1 2 3 4 5	Try to solve many golf technical problems at a time.
Do things slowly.	1 2 3 4 5	Do things quickly.
Express feelings through 'I' messages.	1 2 3 4 5	Do not express feelings.
Have many interests.	1 2 3 4 5	Have few interests outside of golfing.

Total points ___multiply by 3 = ____ Final Score

A golfer who has a Type A+ personality is at much greater risk of heart disease and heart attacks, while a Type B may be at risk of cancer. There is no one perfect personality type which equals a better golfer. Personalities are a critical factor when assessing personal stress levels.

Final Score	Personality Type
75 or more	A+
66 to 74	A
62 to 65	A-
56 to 61	B+
55 and below	B

If you are stressed, you may need to look at yourself, and see what behaviour and parts of your personality will need to change so you can be healthier and happier. Perhaps a Type B may need to become more competitive, and a Type A needs to slow down.

Golf Psyche pre-test

The objective here is to explore your present level of performance. Score your performance now for each category. Complete the chart below as follows:

1. A-J and putter through driver — Evaluate yourself on a scale of 1 (low) to 10 (high), based on how you really are, not on how you would like to be.
2. Fill in your present handicap and average number of putts per round.
3. Self-evaluate your accuracy with a putter, sand wedge, wedge, and chipping, and record your distance yardage.

Categories

Fitness

A.	Muscular strength	1–2–3–4–5–6–7–8–9–10
B.	Flexibility	1–2–3–4–5–6–7–8–9–10
C.	Endurance	1–2–3–4–5–6–7–8–9–10
D.	Diet (eating habits)	1–2–3–4–5–6–7–8–9–10
E.	Sleep habits	1–2–3–4–5–6–7–8–9–10
F.	Knowledge of golf (rules)	1–2–3–4–5–6–7–8–9–10
G.	Technical knowledge of golf	1–2–3–4–5–6–7–8–9–10
H.	Pre-shot routine	1–2–3–4–5–6–7–8–9–10
I.	Ability to control life stress	1–2–3–4–5–6–7–8–9–10
J.	Ability to control golf stress	1–2–3–4–5–6–7–8–9–10

		Average Yardage Range
Pitching Wedge	1–2–3–4–5–6–7–8–9–10	_____ to _____
Sand wedge	1–2–3–4–5–6–7–8–9–10	_____ to _____
Chipping	1–2–3–4–5–6–7–8–9–10	_____ to _____
Nine iron	1–2–3–4–5–6–7–8–9–10	_____ to _____
8	1–2–3–4–5–6–7–8–9–10	_____ to _____
7	1–2–3–4–5–6–7–8–9–10	_____ to _____
6	1–2–3–4–5–6–7–8–9–10	_____ to _____
5	1–2–3–4–5–6–7–8–9–10	_____ to _____
4	1–2–3–4–5–6–7–8–9–10	_____ to _____
3	1–2–3–4–5–6–7–8–9–10	_____ to _____
2	1–2–3–4–5–6–7–8–9–10	_____ to _____
1	1–2–3–4–5–6–7–8–9–10	_____ to _____
5-wood	1–2–3–4–5–6–7–8–9–10	_____ to _____
4-wood	1–2–3–4–5–6–7–8–9–10	_____ to _____
3-wood	1–2–3–4–5–6–7–8–9–10	_____ to _____
Driver	1–2–3–4–5–6–7–8–9–10	_____ to _____
Additional clubs		
_____	1–2–3–4–5–6–7–8–9–10	_____ to _____
_____	1–2–3–4–5–6–7–8–9–10	_____ to _____

Present skill level (handicap _____)

Putter — number of putts per round _____

Self-assessment: Mark with * the areas that you want to have an additional focus on.

Course management

When you develop a golf plan, you develop a template for course management. I recommend you analyze and study your course, dissect it, and factor in club selections, weather, advantage location, and trouble spots to avoid. On the template below, plan your shot target, clubs selection, angle of approach, pin placement, and areas to avoid. Use the legend to plan out your address and approach to the hole, to provide a visual shot plan of target and ball placement.

Most courses that have competitive tournaments will have a detailed package that provides exact yardage markings. Green evaluation and the daily green shot will tell you where the pin placement is. I suggest you still use this process to start to script in success and visual preparation of the target.

Golf Psyche Course Management Planning			
Course		Rating	Date
Hole No.	Yardage	Weather Forecast	
Tee ☐		Green FL ☐ BL C FR ☐ BR	
1st Shot Club Shaping	2nd Shot Club Shaping	3rd Shot Club Shaping	Putt-green speed
Trajectory	Trajectory	Trajectory	Slope

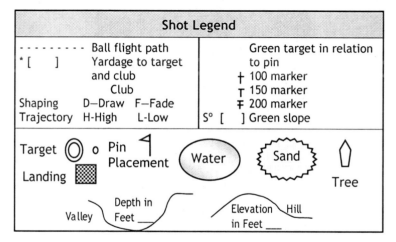

Shot Legend	
- - - - - - - - - Ball flight path * [ ] Yardage to target and club Club Shaping D—Draw F—Fade Trajectory H-High L-Low	Green target in relation to pin † 100 marker ᴛ 150 marker Ŧ 200 marker S° [ ] Green slope

Target ⦿ o Pin Placement ⌐   Water   Sand   Tree

Landing ▦

Valley   Depth in Feet ___   Elevation in Feet ___ Hill

Your conscious brain

In the opening chapters, we discussed the conscious and unconscious brains in great detail. The conscious brain has a breakdown of two parts, as shown in the diagram below.

It is important to be aware of which side you use more. A golfer with a right-side dominant brain will usually not pay attention to making plans of what to do, and will be more likely to be a risk taker on a course, while a player with a left side dominant brain will have a really logical game plan. A person with a highly dominant left brain will have a difficult time changing their plans, but because golf is a game of mistakes, as was noted earlier, there is a need to be flexible and creative.

Golfers need to understand we all have two sides to our brains, and to learn to be aware of which side is dominant, so that we can become balanced. The best golfers are those who are able to plan their game well, taking into consideration their dominant brain system. Once the golfer is aware of how they function in regard to brain dominance, they can make their game plan fit their style. They also can be aware of how they can use their knowledge to focus on practicing and increasing their ability to incorporate the other part of their brain (e.g., a left brainer who is in a difficult spot can use their right brain to help find a creative way out). With planning in place, the unconscious brain just does what it is told.

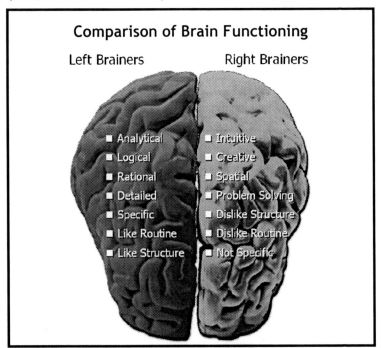

Comparison of Brain Functioning

Left Brainers	Right Brainers
■ Analytical	■ Intuitive
■ Logical	■ Creative
■ Rational	■ Spatial
■ Detailed	■ Problem Solving
■ Specific	■ Dislike Structure
■ Like Routine	■ Dislike Routine
■ Like Structure	■ Not Specific

Oh my! What a hole!

All of us at one time or another have played consistently, until we met our nemesis — the hole. Through conditioning your mind, and practice, you will eventually be able to rely almost totally on your preparation and utilizing the Golf Zone.

Although at times you may still find yourself overwhelmed, and even distracted by a particular hole, by understanding the power of mental focus you can easily overcome personal doubts.

The following technique is a good one to know just in case you have an "Oh my! What a hole" to overcome. It comes from the work of Dr. Tad James.

Getting past what you perceive as a challenging hole

Step 1.   Close your eyes. Think about where you are right now and notice your anxiety.

Step 2.   In your mind's eye, go to a point five minutes after you have successfully completed the hole to your desired outcome.

Step 3.   Come back to *now*, look out towards the hole, and notice if you have any anxiety now, or has it disappeared? Ensure that you see yourself five minutes past the shot and that you are successful.

*Repeat steps 1, 2, and 3 quickly, until the anxiety is gone. It may take 1-15 times, but no matter how many, the anxiety will be gone.

Note: Once you have removed the perceived anxiety and are ready, proceed with your normal pre-shot routine, to move from the Success State to the Focus State to create success.

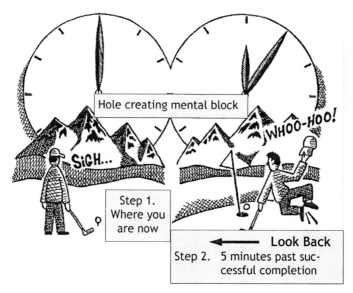

Hole creating mental block

WHOO-HOO!

SiGH...

Step 1.
Where you
are now

Look Back

Step 2.   5 minutes past successful completion

More is not necessarily better

When you practice physically or mentally, more is not always better. Each of us has a tolerance threshold for what will be gained. Each and every exercise needs to have a purpose and objective. Just going through the motions will serve little benefit in improving your performance.

Practice is for getting better, not worse. Too many work when they should be resting. If you find yourself declining, listen to your body and take a well-deserved break. Check out your fun list, and go have some fun.

Accept only what helps when you do it. Practice makes champions! However, over-practice can ruin them! Be smart, have a standard of effort that is acceptable, and when your concentration goes below that level, take a break. Practice to the level of your performance and potential. For example, a pro will practice more than a Friday afternoon golfer. You will need to develop your weekly practice routine and determine how long each of the 40-40-20 periods will be each day to allow you to reach your goals.

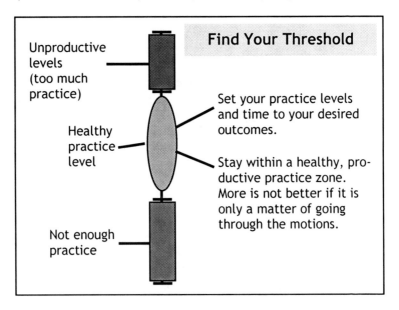

Unproductive levels (too much practice)

Healthy practice level

Not enough practice

Find Your Threshold

Set your practice levels and time to your desired outcomes.

Stay within a healthy, productive practice zone. More is not better if it is only a matter of going through the motions.

The rule of practice is always quality, not quantity.

Have a bounce in your step between shots

When you walk between shots, it's recommended that you be mindful of how you walk, in regard to the following:

 • Body tilt
 • Posture
 • Facial Expression
 • Breathing
 • Walking speed

Anthony Robbins teaches that people who have great body position can create a healthy physiology. As we have discussed, a healthy physiology will have a huge influence on your ability to make your shot. On the course, no matter what happens, you can control how you walk between shots.

Let's test Anthony Robbins' theory.

1. Go to the practice tee and as you walk, put a frown on your face, walk slowly, with your head down, and do this throughout the first 20 shots. Record your results.

2. STOP. Walk away from the practice area, 100 yards, head up, with a huge smile on your face, shoulders back, and walk back to the tee with a confident stride.

3. Now compare the outcomes. Which felt easier to practice with? Which were you more accurate with?

In between shots, no matter the outcome, be aware of how your walk can set up your physiology for the next shot, and help to prepare you for success. The walk of energy and bounce also will help you to continue to create positive emotions. Walk with a smile, for as Tracy teaches, it takes 13 muscles to smile, and over 100 to frown. So save some energy for the course, and smile.

Progressive muscle relaxation

This is an excellent golf stress reduction method to relax muscles, to remove all the tension of the day. Because the body can hold stress, if we relax all of our muscles using this method, we will reduce the stress. Remember, the purpose of health is to have a healthy body and mind. Unwanted stress in our bodies serves no purpose, so let's get rid of this stuff.

Step 1 — Lie down in a comfortable, quiet spot, listening to a peaceful sound, such as ocean waves.

Step 2 — Clench your fists as tightly as possible and hold for 15 seconds, then release. Then clench your fist and forearm; hold for 15 seconds, then release. Add tensing of the biceps, with the same procedure.

Step 3 — Following the above procedure, add your head, face, throat, shoulders.

Step 4 — Add your chest, stomach, lower back.

Step 5 — Add thighs, buttocks, calves, feet, toes.

Step 6 — Clench your entire body for 15 seconds.

Step 7 — Throughout the exercise, notice how relaxed your muscles are, how loose you now feel.

Note: Repeat exercise until you are totally relaxed. I suggest listening to soft music when doing the techniques. There also are tapes that are made for progressive muscle relaxation that are excellent to use, because they have a script read to you and music in the background. This is an alternative to meditation. — Give it a go.

Super Set — This is a term common to athletes. It is when you do one exercise, followed directly by another. I recommend you Super Set progressive muscle relaxation with meditation or guided imagery — and enjoy the benefits!

Dealing with a poor shot

Many of us, when we hit a bad shot, come down hard on ourselves and go into a real negative emotional state, thinking,
everything is wrong with me, almost as if we are instantly a
failure, or a bad person.

Think about the many factors that may have contributed to
your bad shot (e.g., did not follow my pre-shot routine; trying
to correct my swing; not trusting my swing). When you understand the different possible real causes, you will be able to
deal with the disappointment more easily.

The following steps will help you change this thinking:

1. Look at cause and effect connections between your thinking and acting.

2. Examine other factors contributing to it (e.g., instead of
   being no good, you accept the fact that you are human,
   and you forgot to follow a step).

3. Focus on solving the problem, instead of using up energy
   blaming yourself and feeling guilty (e.g., go back to your
   pre-shot routine).

No matter what you do, you cannot solve the problem of a
missed shot. All you can do is ensure it doesn't blow up and
affect your entire round. Too many people throw an entire
round because they get upset and keep cycling the frustration
from one shot into the next, resulting in a poor round.

Dealing With a Poor Shot	
1. Cause	
2. Factors Contributing	
3. Solution	

No one said your swing needs to be perfect

As we discussed, all human beings are fallible, and so are our golf swings. One of the biggest mistakes a golfer can make is to try to correct a golf swing on the course. The conscious thought of trying to make correction will confuse the unconscious mind about what it should do. *So never try to change your golf swing on a golf course.*

To excel at golf, you need to practice, following the 40-40-20 rule. Once you have developed sound swing mechanics, trust your swing. Too many golfers, try to correct a swing 20 minutes before they tee off. This will usually cause the same difficulties as trying to correct it on the course.

A pro like Jack Nicklaus may be able to do this from time to time, but he has six green jackets. I really suggest that until you are close to Nicklaus in experience and skill, save your correction for the practice range and golf lessons.

Tip: Take lessons from a PGA pro or professional golf instructor privately. Develop a sound swing, and use and practice it. As you need to adjust, go back to the same trusted teacher. At all costs, avoid the temptation of listening to all the wonderful tips from your peers on the course and range. Once you start listening to golf tips, the conscious mind will become over-active and confused. If you need a tuneup, like a car, go get one from a place you trust.

Keep it simple — develop one swing, believe in it, and practice it.

Whatever swing you have on a particular day is the swing you have. In your mind, learn to believe that what you have for the day may not be perfect, but that you have to go with it. Adjust mentally, be creative, focused, and devoted to trusting all your practice, and watch the good shots come in.

By being patient and not over-activating your conscious mind with confusion, the unconscious mind may take a couple of holes now and then to get the old swing going. Whether it does, or it doesn't, all you can do is believe and not force it.

In the end, if you believe you do not need to always be perfect, and you trust your swing, you'll be fine.

A few good golf psychology tips

An excellent resource on sports psychology has been written by Timothy Gallwey, called *The Inner Game of Golf*. I have taken four small tips from his work to provide you with a few new tools for golf success. Each technique is intended to help you play golf with more ease and less perceived pressure and tension.

- Back — hit — stop. To help keep club head attention the instant the club is at its perceived highest point, say the word "back," then as you strike the ball, say "hit," and at the top of the swing, say "stop." The purpose is not to analyze your swing, but to get a feel of where your club head is throughout the swing.

- DA-DA-DA-DA. To avoid internal commands while over the ball, you can say "da" while moving away from the ball, "da" at the top of the swing, "da" at the hit phase, and "da" at the top of the swing. It is another great exercise for club head awareness.

- Just hum. If you feel tight, and perceive that your body is stiff and tight, just swing your club, and hum. The principle works on the fact that, by humming, the body will be able to relax, utilizing the hum as a biofeedback mechanism to allow the muscles to relax and become loose. So just keep humming and swinging the club; notice how relaxed your muscles become, and how the tension has been released.

- Golf: It's a game — games are intended to be fun. To become the best you can be, don't focus only on performance outcomes, such as score and victories. The key to golf success is to learn how to trust yourself and be aware of what you are doing and what feels good. In addition to performance, focus on the enjoyment of golf and all the new learnings available. Golf is a game that is played on the outside and won by the game we play on the inside.

100 yards-and-in law

Based on the law of 40-40-20, which I have explained as the ultimate formula for success, let's talk about perception being projection.

Any time a ball is within 100 yards of the hole, it's a mistake not to focus your unconscious mind and conscious mind on it. By saying, *just get it close to the hole* may not be accurate.

What does it specifically mean to get it close? Be careful what you think, and be specific about what you want. Pick a small target.

Practice the **Telescope Projection** method every time, and project mentally where the ball will go, no matter how far away you are from the hole. When you are within 100 yards, do the following every time prior to going through your pre-shot routine:

1. In your mind, project your total focus on exactly where the ball will go. For example: if you have a 20-yard chip, focus on exactly what the ball is going to do and exactly where it's going to go (e.g., into the hole).

2. Project to the ball once again, with an affirmation: "OK, Mr. Ball, have a good trip into the hole." See the ball connected to your club and extend your club, using the telescope technique in your mind, to the exact target (e.g., in the hole).

3. Start your pre-shot routine. When you enter the Focus State, your unconscious mind will take over. It's important that whatever happens, allow your conscious mind to accept the outcome. Just keep your focus and repeat the routine each and every time.

This may sound far out, but with conditioning and focus, you will be amazed at the results.

You cannot entirely control your subconscious mind,
but you can voluntarily hand over to it any plan,
desire or purpose which you wish transformed into concrete form.
— *Napoleon Hill*

I can't keep my cool!

Many golfers lose their temper on a golf course when they don't make a shot they believe they should have. In my early days (teens), I had been known to throw a club! Funny — I can't remember that ever reversing what I had just done. The ball was still in the pond, and my club was in a tree.

It came to me one day that this was a problem, when I was on No. 15, a par-5, in my home town, when my father looked shaken, and I said, "Dad, what's wrong?" And he said, "I don't know what you're going to do next, Bill. You make me nervous."

I was one of those real fun people to play a round of golf with — if I played well, everything was fine. When I was upset, everyone got a part of my pain. You wouldn't know anyone like this, would you?

To overcome this, I needed to make a commitment to stop. I had to make a plan that I would receive more pain for the acting out behaviour than the pain of missing a shot. I thought to myself, "If I was playing golf with the President of the United States, would I throw a club?" Of course not! So I do not have a control problem, I have a choice problem.

If you want to learn how to make healthier choices, follow these steps.

1. *Want* to control your temper — anger.

2. Think of something you find extremely painful to do (e.g., painting, cooking, or a food you dislike).

3. Now think about doing this activity over and over again as many times as you can stand, and then add 10 more times.

4. Now get a bunch of cards made with the statement below, and pass them out to all of your golf buddies, caddies, and family.

If you dare pick a painful enough activity, I assure you, you will only lose your cool a couple of times. If it doesn't work, call me. I'll come up with one I know you will quickly respond to.

Every time I choose to lose my cool on the course, I will:

_____

Name _____ Date _____

Changing your language

Your language is often the cause of sustaining your negative thinking. Language patterns shape your thinking and thinking shapes your language. This technique challenges your self-doubting and unhealthy self-talk or self-messages into more positive and productive ones. Become your own self-calmer. Learn how to talk to yourself in a useful way. Identify your ongoing negative self-talk.

This exercise provides an opportunity to practice changing negative statements into positive statements.

Instead of dwelling on negative messages, gradually turn it into a new positive self-statement, such as:

I can handle this.
Just stay calm — take a deep breath.

Complete the following supporting statement (e.g., It's OK to make mistakes, because golf is a game in which mistakes will happen):

It's OK: to make mistakes

_____

_____

_____

_____

_____

_____

In golf, the ability to create a positive word will assist you to have positive thoughts, which will help keep you in the game.

Practice expressing positive language — and live life positively.
— Bill Howatt

Overcoming mental blocks

The purpose of this exercise is to provide another way to change your internal state when you want to — and thus change your behaviour.

Swish pattern is a technique that allows you to take your unwanted behaviour and switch it with a desired behaviour. Stated below is an explanation of how you can use the technique. For example, if you do not like mental preparation, try this. Read all five steps first, then sit down and *swish* yourself to a new internal state.

Swish pattern

Step 1. Identify the behaviour you want to change or add, then imagine the behaviour in your mind's eye.

Step 2. Create a new picture of what you want, as if you made the desired change, and see yourself doing it.

Step 3. Pretend you are looking at a large movie screen and make a big, bright picture of the unwanted behaviour you want to change (e.g., not doing mental preparation). Now, in front of the unwanted picture, put the desired picture (doing the Success Club) on the screen and then shrink it down to the size of a black postage stamp, in the bottom left-hand corner of your screen. Not yet, but in a moment, be ready to take that small picture and in less than a millisecond have it blow up in size and brightness and literally burst through the picture of the unwanted behaviour, so you no longer can see that one. All you can see is the new picture, with all its excitement and rewards.

Step 4. OK, so are you ready to go? On a count of three, take the small picture and enlarge it, so you can see only the new picture. Ready — 1-2-3 — *Swish it.*

Step 5. Now clear the picture and start all over again from Step 1, repeating this pattern until the picture of the unwanted behaviour disappears, to the point that you can no longer find it.

This is a powerful technique to create the pictures you want and deserve in your head. It will set you on the road to creating new behaviours.

Printed in the United States
202285BV00010B/6/A

9 781894 338806